By the Word of Their Testimony

"And they overcame him because of the
blood of the Lamb and because of the
word of their testimony…"
Revelation 12:11

Rest in the Lord and Wait Patiently for Him

Book 9

Erin Thiele

Cover Design by Dallas & Tara Thiele • NarrowRoad Publishing House

By the Word of Their Testimony

Rest in the Lord and Wait Patiently for Him

By Erin Thiele

Published by:
NarrowRoad Publishing House
POB 830
Ozark, MO 65721 U.S.A.

The materials from Restore Ministries were written for the sole purpose of encouraging women. For more information, please take a moment to visit us at: **EncouragingWomen.org** or **RestsoreMinistries.net**.

Permission from the author has been given to those who wish to print or photocopy this book for themselves or others, strictly for encouragement and informational purposes; however, such copies or reprints cannot be sold in any form without prior written permission from the author.

ISBN: 1-931800-65-0
ISBN 13: 978-1-931800-65-5

Contents

Introduction

Your Divine Appointment

"I was **crying** to the LORD with my voice,
And He **answered me** from His holy mountain"
—Psalm 3:4

Have you been searching for marriage help? It's not by chance, nor is it by coincidence, that you are reading this book. God has heard your cry for help in your marriage dilemma. He predestined this DIVINE APPOINTMENT to give you the hope that you so desperately need right now!

If you have been told that your marriage is hopeless or that without your spouse's help your marriage cannot be restored, then this is the book you need. Read this over and over so you will begin to believe that God is MORE than able to restore ANY marriage, including YOURS!

We know and understand what you are going through since WE, and MANY others who have come to our ministry for help, have a restored marriage and family! No matter what others have told you, your marriage is NOT hopeless!! We KNOW, after twenty five years of ministry, that God is able to restore ANY marriage, even YOURS!

If you have been crying out to God for more help, someone who understands, then join our Internet Restoration Fellowship to help you see your marriage through to restoration during your rebuilding phase of your journey. Since beginning this fellowship, we have seen more marriages restored on a regular basis than we ever thought possible!

So, if you are really serious in your desire to restore your marriage, then our fellowship is the answer. For more information or to join, go to our website RMIEW.com. We would love for you to be a part of our Restoration Fellowship!

Who are we and what are we hoping to do?

Restore Ministries helps those who have found themselves in a hopeless situation: couples whose spouse is in adultery, has left, has filed for divorce, or any other seemingly impossible marital situation. These broken people have often sought help, but everyone (many times even their pastors) have told them their marriage was hopeless. However, we not only believe that no marriage is hopeless – regardless of the circumstances—we know they aren't. That's why we offer hope, help and encouragement through our website, our Restoration Fellowship, and a variety of resources including a variety of newsletters to spiritual feed and uplift you daily!

In 2001, Restoration Fellowship was birthed to minister more effectively to the needs of those seriously seeking restoration. Within a year the fellowship grew to over 400 committed members and increases daily with members from all over the world.

Restore Ministries has never sought advertising or paid for placement in search engines but has instead grown by word of mouth. We also take no support from anyone but the individuals themselves who are seeking restoration so that we are never told we must comprise sharing His full truths. Though often ostracized by the established church, because of those who have cried out to God for help when their own church, pastor, family and friends who offered them no hope or support, we have given them hope and we have become an oasis in the desert for the desperate, the hurting, the rejected.

Often accused of being extreme, radical, out-of-balance or legalistic, the message in all our resources is founded firmly on the Word of God only, encouraging those seeking restoration to live the message that Jesus proclaimed, beginning with the familiar Beatitudes.

RMI teaches the good news of God's Word to bring healing to the brokenhearted, comfort to those in pain, and freedom to prisoners of despondency and sin through the truth of His Word, giving them the hope that is "against all hope" through the Power of Jesus Christ, the Mighty Counselor and Good Shepherd.

Our site and our resources minister to the hurting all over the world with the intent of creating a deeper and more intimate walk with the Lord that results in the hurting healed, the bound freed, the naked clothed, the lost saved and broken marriages restored. We minister to women from more than 15 countries including Switzerland, Hong Kong, New Zealand, Sweden,

Philippines, Brazil and Germany, with large followings in Australia, Canada, and Africa. Our books have been translated into Spanish,

Portuguese, Tagalog (Filipino), Afrikaans, and French. Also Slovakian, Chinese, Russian, Italian and some Hindi.

Jesus said that you "will know them by their fruits" that's why this book and all our *By the Word of Their Testimony* books are filled with testimonies of hopeless marriages that were restored, marriages that give glory to God and to the Power of His Word. Our *WOTT* books are growing at such a phenomenal rate that we were once unable to keep up with getting them published. Now we have a full team devoted to keeping up.

If you have any doubt about the validly of our ministry, you won't after reading this and our other awesome books. Each will show you not only hopeless marriages that were restored, but more importantly, it will show you men and women who have been completely transformed into God-lovers and are now committed on-fire Christians, many of whom were saved through this ministry.

Below is a small sampling of the letters of gratitude that Restore Ministries has received. Please note when you read the letters that they give all the praise and glory to the Lord. This ministry was founded and continues to grow on the premise that "if He be lifted up, He will draw all men to Himself" and "the Lord will share His glory with no man."

"Let Another Praise You" Proverbs 27:2

I don't know where to begin thanking you for your obedience to God in His calling to minister to women and stand in the gap with them for their marriage. Without this course and the materials provided (I also purchased them), I would still be stumbling around trying to figure it all out on my own through prayer. You have helped pave the way and open the door for others to knock, seek, and ask, and through it all, miracles are being performed and lives are forever being changed through and by His grace. During my first 30 days, I have learned how to direct my prayers to seek His will over my own, and in that time, He has shown me more about myself than I ever would have learned by going through this journey without your guidance. I am a new person, but I am not finished growing and learning. I anxiously and eagerly look forward to delving into the next course to grow even closer to my Love.

~ From Tammy in Mississippi

My marriage situation was ABSOLUTELY hopeless, and although I don't want to give too much detail while God is working, the point is PRAISE and GLORY to GOD!! GOD IS WORKING!

Lord Father, I thank You soooo much for holding my hand through this tough season. I know that it is You who has been helping me through everything in this journey. Thank You for guiding me to this page. I love You Lord and I thank You for all the love You show me. In Jesus name.

~ From Jeannine in Texas

When the Lord directed me to this ministry through Restored in Grace I was destroyed, my world had collapsed as a result of my marital destruction, I was devastated in pain, without hope and trying to find an answer as to why and what was happening to me.

Then through looking for God and looking for someone to give me encouragement I found this ministry, when I received the book How God Can and Will Restore Your Marriage I felt a joy that was smiling alone, not only because I saw a hope but because whoever it was He is going to restore is the Lord, and we know that everything he does works for good, knowing that this was a way to draw my attention to him brought me to seek him more and more and my precious Lord every day surprised me more.

~ From Sofia in Dominican Republic

We put this book and all our *Word of Their Testimony* books together because we believe that as you spend some time reading these incredible and awesome testimonies of seemingly hopeless marriages that were miraculously restored, you will be encouraged and know without a doubt...

NOTHING IS IMPOSSIBLE WITH GOD!!

Nothing is Impossible
with God!

"Looking at them, Jesus said,
'With people it is impossible,
but not with God;
for all things are possible with God.'"
Mark 10:27

*"And they overcame him because of the blood of the Lamb and because of the **word of THEIR testimony**, and they did not love their life even to death." Rev. 12:11.*

The following testimonies are filled with miracles of men and women who took God at His Word and believed that "nothing was impossible with God!" Those who have had the miracle of a restored marriage have several things in common. All "delighted themselves in the Lord" and He gave them "the desires of their heart." All of them "hoped against hope" when their situation seemed hopeless.

All of them "fought the good fight" and "finished their course." All of them were determined "not to be overcome with evil" but instead to "overcome evil with good." All were willing to "bless their enemies" and to pray for them that "despitefully used and persecuted them." All "turned the other cheek" and "walked the extra mile." All realized that it was "God who removed lover and friend far from" them and it was God who "made them a loathing" to their spouse. All of them understood and believed that it is NOT the will of man (or woman) but the "will of God" who can "turn the heart" whichever way He chooses.

All refused to fight in "the flesh" but chose to battle "in the spirit." None were concerned to protect themselves, but trusted themselves "to Him who judges righteously." All of their trust was "in the Lord" because their trust was "the Lord." All released their attorneys (if that was part of their testing) since they "would rather be wronged or defrauded." All of them "got out of the way of wickedness" and "let the unbeliever leave" since they "were called to peace." All refused to do "evil for evil or insult for insult." All loved their spouse who may have been unfaithful because they knew that "love never fails."

This is the same journey that the Lord took me on back in 1989. That year I made a promise to God that if He would restore my marriage to my husband, I would devote my life to telling others about Him and His desire and ability to restore ANY marriage no matter what the circumstances. The Lord was faithful and restored my marriage, suddenly, two years later after a divorce. (Yes! AFTER a divorce!) Now I faithfully, with the Lord's continued help, love, support, and guidance, spread the GOOD news that nothing—NOT A THING—is impossible with God!

It is important to know that our ministry was FOUNDED to help all those who were told by pastors and Christian friends that their situations were HOPELESS. Those who come to us for hope are facing a spouse who is deep in adultery, who has moved out (often in with the other man or woman who committed adultery with), who has already filed for divorce or whose divorce has gone through. 99% of those who come, come alone for help since their spouse is not interested in saving their marriage, but is desperately trying to get out. Over 95% claim that they are Christians and most are married to Christians.

Over half are in some type of Christian service and many of the men who are involved with other woman are pastors who have left not only their wife and children, but their church as well.

If you, or if someone you know, is facing devastation in their marriage, there is hope. Read these awesome testimonies that prove that God is MORE than able to restore ANY marriage—even YOURS!

Chapter 1

Courtney

"For God will bring every deed
into judgment, along with every hidden thing,
whether good or evil."
—Ecclesiastes 12:14

"I Became Neurotic"

Courtney, how did your restoration actually begin?

I was a bossy, extravagant woman, arrogant, and I thought that only I could solve all our problems. Even our wedding was a nightmare, due to me wanting a huge wedding party, because I wanted to, and we ended up with an enormous amount of debt that caused a lot of stress. I smoked and drank a lot, and my friends and family had tried to warn me that I needed to change; they tried to get my attention, but I did not care.

Right away, I wanted to get pregnant, and I became neurotic because of that. To cope, my husband started to seclude himself to get away from me; he became quieter and isolated himself from me, until he came to tell me that he was in friendship with a work colleague who had the same job as him, and he claimed that they had to work together. People said it was true, they were only friends and coworkers, but I imagined the worse. After two months of much fighting and distrust on my part, with my continual accusations, my husband decided to leave, to give us time apart to stop the fights. A week later, I decided to go behind his back and ask his boss to transfer him. After sending my husband several messages, he decided that he was done; he would not come home; we were through. He came home, packed up his things without talking to me, and moved out.

How did God change your situation, Courtney, as you sought Him wholeheartedly?

After he had left home and was gone for a month, I was exhausted from running around and just kicking him verbally, telling everyone and anyone who would listen. Each time I tracked him down and he'd see me, the colder he became toward me. A friend told me I needed help and to go see a counselor in her church—such a waste. I could not find any help, and then it came to my mind to look for testimonies of restored marriages online. By that time, I was going to the church and told this to my husband, trying to show him that I had changed (joke) and was urging him to go, too.

I knew I needed God, but I didn't know which direction to take, what course of action would make this all stop—not until He led me right to the RMI website. From the moment I started reading the first HopeAtLast.com pages, I began to cry and stayed up late into the night reading—going from one page to the other. At that moment, I knew that it was God speaking to me, and that's when I ordered and read *How God Can and Will Restore,* and I kept reading the testimonies, then I began working through each of the courses and started reading the daily Encourager.

What principles, from God's Word (or through our resources), Courtney, did the Lord teach you during this trial?

God taught me, through RMI, to have a meek, gentle and loving spirit, to forgive and not to explode at anything, to let my husband lead, instead of taking control of everything, and to remain calm and at peace when I would have been filled with rage and exploded in anger over something stupid. Your ministry continues teaching me to be quiet and let go of everything, turning it all over to His powerful hands. And only then was I able to rest and know that He was taking care of everything. He taught me the principles of tithing and surrendering, which were very, very important, and that was when I finally began to see things change.

What were the most difficult times that God helped you through, Courtney?

The first most difficult time was when I let go of my EH and confessed my sins to him and others (including a kiss that a guy gave me at the beginning of our engagement). I learned to let go of my life and stop contacting him, which was tough when I found out about him and OW.

Up until that day, I only suspected that he had gone out with her, even though people told me they were together. Even without children, we had contact throughout, due to our bank accounts.

One day, he came and confessed that after we separated that he went out with her once but that he had repented to God. So that day we had intimacy, but after, he said we should not have done it, because he was afraid to hurt me, but that showed me that the Lord was beginning to turn his heart back to me even more, so I focused on the positive.

The second most difficult moment was when he was sleeping at home and he got a text from the OW saying that she took a test and she was pregnant. That day our world collapsed, but I felt God talking to me to remain calm and trust Him, and I asked, "But how can I stay calm with this news? If it is Your will that the dream of my husband being a father be performed by another woman, I will understand." But as I became more intimate with the Lord as my Husband, I kept hearing Him tell me that not everything was what it seemed, and the more I wondered if it was true.

More tests were sent by God, and the more wonderful Lord continued to give me peace. After several crises, the truth surfaced; we discovered that the sonograms she sent to prove she was pregnant were four years old.

But before we discovered the pregnancy was not my husband, my EH had returned to his sister's house, and he said he needed to decide what to do about our future together. I kept talking to my HH, and I went on fasting and praying, and that's when the heavenly peace of my Beloved consumed me. One day, I even told my EH that he should also trust God and that His will be done but that I thought she was not pregnant. God had not revealed the truth, but I thought "either she would abort or it was a lie," and it was the next day the truth was uncovered. After this, my EH came to sleep at home but said to remain quiet.

The OW did not know that we knew the sonogram pictures were old, so he quietly called her to talk, and she told him that she had an abortion, because there was a problem in the womb, but my EH did not confront her about her lie. Though, I confess that I wanted everyone to know that she faked her pregnancy and that we knew that the sonogram was old. But God taught me to remain quiet and trust Him. Later, I realized that maybe the scandal would hurt us as a couple.

Courtney, what was the "turning point" of your restoration?

The turning point was to confess and ask forgiveness from my husband and others I hurt, to speak of my HH about everything, to rejoice in good or bad and be kind to everyone, to dedicate myself only to the Lord, and to stop running after my husband. To be loving and to be quiet, after all these changes is when my EH came back to begin sleeping at home and began to make plans for us, financially and as a family, but always asking me to remain calm. It wasn't until he brought all his uniforms home that I knew things had turned. His excuse was always because (as we live in an apartment) it takes more time for them to dry, and sometimes he had to go two days wearing the same one. I said nothing, and soon he said it was better to bring everything home, and I smiled. The next day, we went to get his things, and he packed everything, leaving nothing behind. All this to the glory and honor of my Beloved Husband!

Tell us HOW it happened, Courtney. Did your husband just walk in the front door? Courtney, did you suspect, or could you tell you were close to being restored?

God was turning his heart slowly; what I see today is so much better and not as I imagined. I always did everything quickly and pushed things to be finished. Yet yesterday, I realized how calm I felt, due to what you taught me here. What a blessing it is to wait and be patient, and I thank you very much. I am able to thank Him for all the trials, because every tear, every bad moment, served to help me and teach me.

Of course, we messed up a lot during the journey, and we are going to make mistakes, but I believe that the important thing is always to seek Him, and what He wants for our lives, and to feel that peace in the heart that only He can give us, even in the midst of the storm. Knowing that He is with us is the most comforting feeling there is! It's been eleven months since the day we came home after picking up his things, and that day he asked me if we were going to start going church! Glory to God!!!

After I let go of my church, as you all teach (so my husband would have room to become my spiritual leader), I confess I thought that would never happen. How wrong I was!

Would you recommend any of our resources in particular that helped you, Courtney?

I recommend that you read *How God Can and Will Restore Your Marriage* and also *A Wise Woman* and purchase them to give as gifts to family and friends. The courses were what helped me a lot, to keep moving forward; as I journaled relentlessly, it helped me not remain just going around and around what I was learning. Just follow each course in the list, plus other recommended courses like Abundant Life. Of course, include a lot of prayers, fasting, and trying to be close to your HH, and do His will and not ours.

Would you be interested in helping encourage other women, Courtney?

Yes

Either way, Courtney, what kind of encouragement would you like to leave women with, in conclusion?

Beloved ones, believe, trust and hope in His promises. Sometimes we think about giving up on our journey, because it is very difficult, but we should not take our eyes off our Beloved; only He can strengthen us. There were days that I asked my HH to take my EH from my heart; I wanted to live only for Him and with Him. It was more due to not wanting to suffer or hurt anymore, but those were not my Heavenly Husband's plans.

Sometimes, I fell asleep in the midst of the tears, and there were many cold nights before He became my HH. But the next day, as I snuggled next to Him, I'd receive good news or little pamperings that my Beloved gave me. Each time I needed it, He filled me with love and hope again.

So, turn to Him; do not give up; as Erin said, even the cases that everyone judges as hopeless are the very ones that He uses to show His power and Glory. I love my Husband and thank God for taking me to the desert and helping me pass through everything I went through. Everything I lived was a lesson taught by the best Teacher of the universe...He is the great I Am! I will be eternally grateful to Him, and I have promised (even before restoration) that I will help as many women as I can. This trial has been wonderful for me as a woman, mother, wife, and daughter, because now I want to do everything for Precious, for my Beloved.

Chapter 2

Ruby

"You have removed lover and friend
far from me; My acquaintances
are in darkness."
—Psalm 88:18

"He Was Disgusted With Me"

Ruby, how did your restoration actually begin?

Hello Brides! I dreamed of the day I would see my testimony on this site, and Praise the Lord, this day has come!

My heart is to share with you some details of my testimony, focusing more on my attitude, rather than exposing my husband. Ever since my journey began, I've searched for a similar testimony as mine, and I have yet to find one. So for quite a while, I thought that perhaps my situation meant that my marriage would not be restored. But now I know that ALL marriages can be blessed with a restoration, Glory to God, because He promises nothing is impossible for Him!

I have been married for 15 years, plus another 4 years when I dated my husband. Our relationship has always had its ups and downs, but I really believed we were both happy. During this time, my husband actually cheated on me a few times, but I always found out. I also ended up cheating on him, but he never discovered my betrayal. Since he didn't know about my sin, I kept pointing to his, whenever we had an argument, and using his betrayals to manipulate him to do what I wanted him to do. As a result, I became the leader of our home; my husband was totally dependent on me, and I foolishly believed, "Our my marriage will only end if I want it to." I was spiritually contentious and arrogant, because I had been a "Christian" much longer than he had been. But the only thing I was more of was being more of a hypocrite—because all my actions were contrary to what God's Word tells us and how we should behave if we are a follower and a believer!

How foolish I was, and as a result, I almost destroyed my marriage forever. Yet God in His infinite mercy rescued me, and I began the true transformation in my life, starting it in the worst way I had imagined: God taking my husband from me.

"You [God] have removed lover and friend far from me; My acquaintances are in darkness" (Psalm 88:18). "You [God] have removed my acquaintances far from me; You have made me an object of loathing to them; I am shut up and cannot go out" (Psalm 18:8).

It happened in December, when I began to notice my husband's different attitude towards me. A man who had always been very affectionate, caring and romantic was now completely frustrated with me and treating me strangely. Over Christmas, I called him at work, just to talk and to ask him what was going on, and I heard what I didn't really expect: "I don't know if I love you anymore." My God, what did he mean?! He was always madly in love with me; it was impossible for me to be hearing those words. Immediately, my world fell—I cursed; I fought; I tried to blackmail him, but nothing shook him. So I realized that this was very serious. He said there was no woman involved, but I had a hard time believing it. We were still married, but our relationship was horrible. My husband no longer said that he loved me, gave me nothing emotionally, left home every night and came back only at dawn, without saying a word to me. To make him stop, I was always fighting, arguing, wanting to argue. But by February, he said he would be moving to another place to live, because he thought it would be better to take a break from living with me.

How did God change your situation, Ruby, as you sought Him wholeheartedly?

My transformation started on a vacation that I had already booked with my daughter and a few of my friends. I went, even though my husband said he would not come as planned. During this trip, I had a true encounter with God. He directed me to read the book *How God Can and Will Restore Your Marriage* that someone had sent me, telling me it was what she was reading. (Which I now see as so brave, because she sent it to all her friends, and none of us knew she and her husband were having marriage issues.) God gave this to me as a sign that I, too, needed to make sure it was not the end of my marriage, and after reading it, I was confident that God would change my situation. Instantly, I understood that God had taken my husband from me, so that He could make a real transformation in my life. Glory to God for rescuing me from the world of deception and opening my eyes!! I plunged headlong into the book.

When I came to the part stating that if I had committed adultery against my husband that I needed to confess it to him, I became really annoyed. Yet, God wouldn't let me go, and I began to feel I was being crushed. Under the weight, I came to realize that everything we were going through was due to my unconfessed sin of betrayal. I began to see God dealing with me, because from that moment I could only see my sins and how foolish I had been until that moment. God showed me that this situation had been created by Him to transform my life, and to do so He also needed to show me how to move my marriage from the sinking quicksand, to rebuild it steadily on the Rock.

"'For I know the plans that I have for you,' declares the LORD, 'plans for welfare and not for calamity to give you a future and a hope'" (Jeremiah 29:11).

"That men may know from the rising to the setting of the sun that there is no one besides Me. I am the LORD, and there is no other, the One forming light and creating darkness, causing well-being and creating calamity; I am the LORD who does all these" (Isaiah 45:6–7).

"Therefore everyone who hears these Words of Mine, and acts upon them, may be compared to a wise man, who built his house upon the rock. And the rain descended, and the floods came, and the winds blew, and burst against that house; and yet it did not fall, for it had been founded upon the rock. Everyone who hears these words of Mine and does not act on them, will be like a foolish man who built his house on sinking sand" (Matthew 7:24-25).

What principles, from God's Word (or through our resources), Ruby, did the Lord teach you during this trial?

The main principles were letting go, to win without words, to possess a meek and quiet spirit and especially to bring all things first to God and never to speak to friends, pastors, etc...as I used to do.

What were the most difficult times that God helped you through, Ruby?

Even though I knew all the principles in the book (after reading it so many times and even after going through the course and journaling), I couldn't control my tongue, nor follow the principle of winning without a word. After coming back from my vacation, my husband didn't talk about leaving home but kept treating me like I didn't exist, so just like the contentious woman I'd always been, I started confronting him!

Oh, how foolish and how painful when we do things we learn are wrong. Dear Bride, please don't do this, Beloved Ones; it only brings even more pain. What Erin says is true—the war will only be won WITHOUT WORDS (and you will read later how true it is).

So, by confronting, I heard from my husband's mouth and saw in his face that he really didn't love me anymore, that he didn't miss me while I was gone, and he told me flat-out that he had no desire to be with me anymore. By confronting him, those words of his entered my heart like a spear, their hurt went deep into my soul, and I ended up reacting— letting my anger speak more loudly due to the pain. Rather than doing it the right way, I blurted out and tried to hurt him by telling my husband about my adultery, not in order to humbly confess, but to hurt! Telling him was all based on anger, not by His Gentle Spirit. When we confess our sins, it cannot be motivated by anger, because God will not be part of this nonsense. We must pray and ask God for the best time and for Him to provide an opportunity to confess (just as the book and courses tell us).

Once I shouted this "confession," my husband stood up from the couch, packed his bags and left the house. From then on, I faced the most difficult times. I heard from him the harshest words I have ever heard in my life from anyone; among the many was my husband saying that he was disgusted with me, that he would never look in my face again, that he would never touch me again, and he even said that he was going back to one of his previous lovers. If there is a description for the "valley of the shadow of death," I say that this day I tumbled headlong into this valley. The pain I experienced, the deep desire to die, the longing to disappear from the face of the earth, begging God to allow me to sleep and to wake me up only when the nightmare was all over, that was something I never thought I'd face—not in a million years!

To add to my pain, the enemy who once accused me of committing adultery now accused me of stupidly confessing my adultery, and this enemy said that because I confessed that my marriage was over; it had no chance of ever being healed. It's such a lie. God honors those who do the right thing, and though I didn't do it the right way, but entirely the wrong way, even then this principle is powerful.

God says in 1 John 1:9, "If we confess our sins, He is faithful and righteous to forgive us our sins and to cleanse us from all unrighteousness." And "He who covers his transgressions shall not prosper" (Proverbs 28:13). He is true to His Word!

Ruby, what was the "turning point" of your restoration?

The turning point was when I started taking the "Hope at Last" course. I decided that this time I would apply all the principles, as painful as each seemed. The very next day, I began to see God acting in my life. The day after my EH said those horrible words I quoted above, I remained silent and praying as he said those words for a second time. Because I said nothing, he finished by saying that he was contacting a lawyer and to be ready for his lawyer to contact me. He said that he wanted me to sign the divorce papers that week. Again, I didn't reply, just nodded, and I kept praying, trusting Him to battle for me!

"Do not fear! Stand by and see the salvation of the Lord which He will accomplish for you today..." (Exodus 14:13).

Before he left, I went to give him a hug; he resisted and stepped back. So again, I said nothing, nodded that I understood, but then suddenly he turned around and hugged me, which led to us being intimate. Glory to God, within minutes of hearing that he was disgusted with me for the second time, God rewarded my obedience! My hope was igniting even more and even more; I witnessed how powerful His principles are.

After we were intimate, my EH left the house and didn't tell me where he was going, and this time I let him go (following the letting go principle). It wasn't just that I didn't try to stop him or follow him, I followed the principle in my heart, which is where God sees and what He looks at. "I, the Lord, search the heart, I test the mind, even to give to each man according to his ways, according to the results of his deeds" (Jeremiah 17:10). I honestly didn't care, which is why I didn't ask anything at all. I, instead, was glad he was gone, so I could dive deeper into the courses. I read the book again, for the fifth time, moved on to Courses 2 and 3, and I started reading the Bible through, using the recommended app. I began fasting, and I gave my life completely to the Lord—which is when He became my Savior for the first time!

I called myself a Christian, because I went to church, but I don't believe I was one until this moment. I began to have a relationship with the Lord for the first time in my life. I put Him first in my life, and soon He became my first Love, my Heavenly Husband.

The next morning, after my Beloved and I became Lovers, my EH texted me, telling me that he would forgive me and that he would never talk about it again, and he also would never again talk about divorce— glory to God! From that day on, my EH came to visit us regularly (we have an 8-year-old son), and sometimes we were intimate, but for the most part, he remained very cold and distant from me. But by this time, the rejection no longer hurt; I had a Lover, and I would simply give it to my HH and knew it was in God's hands.

Two weeks after my husband had left home, God put in my heart to fast for favor for 3 days, starting on Friday and ending on Sunday. Then at the end of the fast, I was to start praying with my son for 7 days at 6 am, because the word of the Lord says that "I love those who love me, and those who seek me at dawn will find me" (Proverbs 8:17). It says, "Because where two or three are together in my name, I am there with them" (Matthew 18:20). So before he got ready for school, I prayed different promises aloud, and my son said "amen," agreeing with me. We started this campaign on Sunday, and by Monday—my husband showed up at home unexpectedly, and he slept at home all week! From that day on, he slept at home during the week, but on weekends he slept elsewhere. (I never knew and still don't, and of course, I didn't ask.) Talk about building my son's faith in prayer and in God doing the impossible!!!

As far as our restoration, he was practically back; he just had to bring his suitcase home. But when our victory is coming, the enemy gets desperate and changes his focus, trying to make us give up. His scheme was when I found out something after my husband's partial return, about two weeks into it. A "friend" made it a point of contacting me, telling me that my husband was with another woman. He'd been with her for 6 months. She said she was very afraid of how I'd react when I heard this news. She thought for sure I would be devastated, but God was already preparing me for that unwelcomed conversation, and when I received the news I was able to thank her, and then I hung up and rejoiced—because I knew the time was getting closer. Also for the practicality of it, I knew I had much more time to be alone with my HH, and that made my heart soar!

The next scheme the enemy tried (because the first scheme didn't affect me but resulted in pure joy) was him using my husband to say words that were intended to worry or hurt me. My EH told me that he would never, ever step into a church again, that he hated all Christians (because they were all hypocrites) and that all Christians were miserable believers and lived with a broken life. He said he'd never seen a prosperous believer and that he would never again tithe or give an offering in order to make pastors rich. I started a fast this very day, and of course, God had the last word on this too!!

Tell us HOW it happened, Ruby. Did your husband just walk in the front door? Ruby, did you suspect or could you tell you were close to being restored?

My husband left home again for a while, when my son was away staying with relatives, but I continued to rejoice—applying all the principles I learned here, and I told him that I would not stand in his way. (Things, of course, got fierce, because we were so close, as Erin prepares us to remember.) A few weeks passed, but then one day he just showed up with all of his things. He has been living at home with my son and me for over nine months now.

The truth is, I don't know if he still has contact with OW; he never told me about her. (I only knew from my "friend.") I believe that often he used to make up stories, and even though I knew he was lying, I never confronted him, because "love believes all things," and the bottom line is that I know God knows and is in control. I also know that my HH doesn't want me to be hurt (though, with Him, I never could be).

Each time, I just turned any problem or concern to my HH and then focused on living as His bride. Is it easy? No, it wasn't easy every time. Sometimes I thought I was silly, weak, cowardly, but God showed me that shutting up was proof that I was being strong, because it is not easy for you to choke on your own flesh to live literally from the spirit. God told me that by not knowing if he was through with the OW, He was giving me an even greater testimony, and that's why my EH did not return as I expected.

"For among them are those who enter into households and captivate silly women weighed down with various impulses, always learning and never able to come to the knowledge of Truth" 2 Timothy 3:6-7.

I've come to realize that during our restoration journey, we end up idealizing a husband's return. That's based on fairytales, but I realize that in almost all the testimonies I've read in all the books that does not happen. Yet, there's a real reason why God doesn't complete the restoration the moment a husband walks through the door. It's just too easy to go back to your old ways; we each need the motivation to make us want to continue to fast, continue to do our lessons, continue to wake early to spend time alone with our HH.

Whether or not he says he loves me (yet thankfully doesn't treat me like he used to, so I don't try to take control again), today I'm a different woman, a different wife. Instead of complaining that he comes home late, I thank my HH, because he's coming home, and I have more time alone with Him. Everything is something to rejoice over, whether it's good or bad. It's a beautiful way to live! My life and my husband's life are being rebuilt and grounded in the Rock, and we are no longer on the sinking sand.

Even though my husband said he'd never step into a church again, that all Christians were hypocrites, miserable, broken, not prosperous, and that he would never again tithe or give an offering in order to make pastors rich, the week he returned and asked about why I was tithing, and I told him about my storehouse, giving him the chapter on *Opening the Windows of Heaven* for men, he began to tithe to RMI too!!!

Would you recommend any of our resources in particular that helped you, Ruby?

I recommend reading and owning the books *How God Can and Will Restore Your Marriage* and *A Wise Woman*. Then just follow the restoration journey map, and go through all your online courses.

Would you be interested in helping encourage other women, Ruby?

For sure!!

Either way, Ruby, what kind of encouragement would you like to leave women with, in conclusion?

Be sure to continue to apply all the principles, especially to win without words. Also, I ask absolutely nothing of my EH, nor do I question him in any way, as I learned in *A Wise Woman*. Instead, I know I have a HH and a Heavenly Father who will take care of all my needs. I know that I will know what God wants me to know, and whatever my EH does not tell me, I know that God is saving me from any pain. I am no longer the silly foolish woman I used to be. "For among them are those who enter into households and captivate silly women weighed down with various impulses, always learning and never able to come to the knowledge of Truth" (2 Timothy 3:6-7).

As most testimonies attest to after a husband returns home—it gets much harder, not easier, because applying the principles with him living here is much more difficult. Yet, I'm so thankful for all of this.

YES, my marriage is RESTORED, even though the enemy often tries to put in my mind that it's not (because it's not the way I dreamed it would be). So to each of you brides, it's lovely to dream about restoration, the fairytale version, but just as marriage wasn't the fairytale we'd imagined, neither is restoration. Just remember that you CAN be more than happy where you are NOW, in the midst of your journey, even when everything looks hopeless, when you have a Lover.

Learn to live with Him now; then when you are restored, and all throughout your journey, you will find the abundant life and live it for the rest of your life. From the moment that my HH became everything I wanted, everything I needed, and became the reason for my living—nothing else mattered—and the pain was gone—replaced with sheer joy!

To the woman who is reading my testimony, I pray to God that the next testimony is yours and that reading mine right now will help you reach for the life I am living!!! DON'T GIVE UP, EVER, FOR NOTHING IS IMPOSSIBLE FOR GOD!!!

Chapter 3

Génesis

"Leave the presence of a fool
or you will not discern
words of knowledge"
—Proverbs 14:7

"Everything Changed Once I Had My Own Lover!"

Génesis, how did your restoration actually begin?

Soon after my husband and I were married, we moved to a country where I knew no one, because my husband was transferred for his work. I had no family support, and we were going through some financial problems. Because I was a college student, I didn't offer to help by getting part time work, as he'd asked. As my classes increased, I started to be gone almost all day, and it was overwhelming me too much. My husband did all the cooking and cleaning, so I could study at night.

My husband appeared to be showing me that he understood that my schedule would not remain as busy as this, and that soon everything would get better, and I would be home again to spend time with him and do my part. Often, he said sometimes he felt ALONE, but I didn't think that he had gone so far as to seek love and support from someone else.

It was at the end of the school term when things got worse. By mid-summer (I was taking fewer classes, but I was still unable to be home.), things got very difficult. He started saying that he was thinking of someone else and that nothing had yet happened (though later I found out he was very involved), but he assured me these feelings would soon pass. Instead, things just got much worse. I became desperate and sought help from our pastor (who had preached that early in his marriage he had a problem like this). My hope was that my EH would confess to the pastor what he was tempted to do (but actually had done), and then things would be better. But that did not happen, and everything was getting worse and worse.

If I could go back and be the wise woman I am today, I would drop out of school and keep my commitment to be a wife that had I promised when we married. And if I suspected anything, rather than uncover my husband's nakedness and confess his sins to our pastor, I would speak only to my Heavenly Husband, Who would have guided me. But I was a foolish woman who tore her house down; I lacked a gentle and quiet spirit, therefore I reaped what I'd sown.

A month later, I found out everything by going through his email. I read all the conversations he had with the OW, details I can never erase from my mind. Several of my college friends assured me this was the only way, to go snooping into his private emails, so I could catch him. I was listening to and surrounding myself with fools, rather than an older, wiser woman who'd faired well in her own marriage. "Leave the presence of a fool or you will not discern words of knowledge" (Prov. 14:7).

Heartbroken, I read their plans that they were already making to be together, and how he'd planned to leave me. If I hadn't been foolish enough, I confronted him and told him to get out! Where else would he go than to be with the OW? Oh how we continue to fall in step with the enemy's schemes due to our lack of knowledge. (Hos. 4:6) (2 Cor. 2:10–11).

I thank God that in the church that I was attending at the time (I later let go of my church), there were many restoration stories that gave me hope, because I was in the midst of despair. I was very encouraged to continue to seek God for my own restoration, but what I didn't realize is that restoration meant I had to change. I had to know what God expected of me as a wife, woman and bride to my own HH.

So, doing this in my own strength with hope alone, I tried, but I just gave up several times. One day, I decided to get more help on the Internet and saw a video where the girl talked about the book *Restore Your Marriage*. In desperation, I went to look for the book immediately, and that's when I discovered RMI. Just as it says, I found HopeAtLast.com!

This is when everything started to change, because I started to see that it wasn't just me that was going through this journey; there were so many other women who I identified with. Before finding out about RMI, I had decided to quit my job, because I was unable to work; since I was a saleswoman and had to always be smiling, but due to my marriage collapsing, I was so very angry and bitter. I continually thought of the emails I'd read. At that part of my journey, I honestly thought I had done nothing wrong, that I was perfect and without sin!

It was after finding RMI and as I started reading the *A Wise Woman* book, the more and more I realized it was me. I had torn my house down. I had gone after the knowledge of good and evil (because university courses don't teach God's Word but often are opposing it); this I understood after reading "Helper Suitable" in *A Wise Woman*, that I had chosen university knowledge over my marriage vows that I had made before God. I was blind to my sins, and even after reading a lot of your books, I still did a lot of wrong and still did not understand that everything I was learning was for my good. I still did not understand that God loved me, and I felt sorry for myself.

It happened while taking the first Abundant Life course, Finding the Abundant Life; this was when I could feel and understand His love. God revealed this to me, when I finally understood how wrong I was—wrong about things I didn't even know were as serious as they were. God began showing me that I was a lukewarm believer, at best. I saw that I was only looking to God in the difficult times, and when everything got better, I'd immediately forgotten all about Him. I was a contentious, proud woman. I always had an answer on the tip of my tongue, and I would spew it out. Like many university students, I refused to be under any authority, which included my husband. So every conversation turned out to be a big fight that I had to win.

No matter how wrong I'd been, every time I started trying to put the principles of the books and courses into practice, as long as I kept asking God to help me, I began to change. I understood that all this was so much more than fixing a failed marriage. He had allowed it for my good, so that I could experience an intimate relationship with my FIRST LOVE. I began to feel the love of the Lord surround me. I started to realize that, when I was home alone (I'd dropped out of university at this point), that time was to be closer to MY FIRST LOVE. I cried out in a loud voice, humiliated by the pain of realizing my ignorance and sins. I started asking God to change me, because I didn't want to be the same contentious, foolish woman I had been, full of worldly knowledge. I started reading Psalms 119, because in one of the posts in the Encourager, another bride said she read it often and that it helped a lot. So I started reading Psalms and Proverbs aloud daily, falling in love with the Psalms as His love letters to me.

I studied the Proverbs that enriched my life — better than any university course I could take, because it taught me about life!

As I grew spiritually, no longer did God need to make me a loathing or remove my lover and friend. My EH was fine now; he no longer treated me badly. At one point, he asked for forgiveness, not once, but twice, and twice I told him I forgave him for his unfaithfulness. Nevertheless, he would go out and do the same thing again and again. But God started showing me, through the RMI materials (in one of the Abundant Life courses), that I didn't need, nor should I expect, anything from my EH, because he didn't have what I needed.

All I truly needed was my FIRST LOVE. I started calling Him my Beloved; soon after, my LOVE showed me something strange had happened. I always had a deep rooted fear of being disrespected, but as I came closer and closer to my HH, I realized I didn't need any respect; I didn't need anything at all. I had all I needed in Him, and I found myself at perfect peace and rest for my soul. I didn't need a better education, a higher paying job, or for others to think or speak well of me. I had it all; what a paradise it was to live this way!

A week before my restoration, my EH spent the whole week at home, did not go out, and though I was enjoying his company, not expecting anything from him, I missed my time with my HH.

God is wonderful! Today, after being restored for a few months, I know that I had taken God out of His rightful place in my life. I did everything wrong. As a result, I suffered a lot, until I realized that all things work together for good to those who love God. Over the course of my journey, I lost a lot of weight, and I did absurd things (at first), but God took care of me, sent people who know His power, and gave me this wonderful ministry — which has helped me so much to know Him as the Lover of my soul. I even learned to love reading the Bible. I used the recommended app and read through the Bible several times, because the hunger for knowledge must also include wisdom "And beside this, giving all diligence, add to your faith, virtue and to your virtue, knowledge" (2 Pet. 1:5 KJV). I found that even though I could not do what He wants (on my own), when you ask your FIRST LOVE to be your EVERYTHING, then GOD will give you wisdom that is beyond what this world knows or seeks after.

No one will never take His place in my life; every day I can learn more, to do His will for my life, His plans for my life.

My journey lasted just six months—to undo what had taken me six years to demolish. Yet rather than regret or feel shame, now I know that everything works together for good for the honor and glory of the Lord. I can feel His love more and more each day—love that I can feel surrounding me, filling me—because His love transcends me. I love You, My Beloved, my first and only love.

How did God change your situation, Génesis, as you sought Him wholeheartedly?

Yes, as I sought Him with all my heart, He changed everything.

What principles, from God's Word (or through our resources), Génesis, did the Lord teach you during this trial?

I learned the principles of not being a contentious woman, believing against all hope, and believing this was His plan, so I learned to keep His commandments. Most importantly, I learned to seek an intimate relationship with my HH—putting Him in His rightful place, the first in my heart as I continue my lifelong journey with Him.

What were the most difficult times that God helped you through, Génesis?

The times before my intimacy with my HH were most difficult, times I felt so alone, and when my EH said there would never be a marriage for us anymore and that I was crazy. But again, everything changed once I had my own Lover!

Génesis, what was the "turning point" of your restoration?

The turning point was when I began the first of all of your Abundant Life courses. I was able to let go and began to win my husband without a word, when I no longer cared about what anyone else said. Oh, this was when I began wanting His knowledge and wisdom, not seeking it from the higher learning of this world. Now I am happily a *worker@home,* and I am able to minister to other women, so they don't make the mistakes I've made. I also noticed a turn, when I began tithing to my storehouse, so the devourer was not allowed to steal my husband and marriage.

Tell us HOW it happened, Génesis. Did your husband just walk in the front door? Génesis, did you suspect or could you tell you were close to being restored?

One day, he just came over. There was no real sign, but I wasn't looking for one either. I'd come to the place that I'd read so many times in *By the Word of Their Testimonies*, but I honestly never believed I would feel—that I didn't want to be restored, because I was so happy with my life as it was. I believe it was Erin who said this first. He'd slowly been bringing things with him when he'd stop by (which became more and more often), and then that night he asked if he could stay over. I said, "Of course," but I had to ask my HH to give me His love to love my husband with. Well, that is all it took for my EH to feel the Lord's love flowing through me. The next morning, he asked if it was okay for him to stay, if I thought we had a good chance, and I said, "Yes, God will complete what He started in both of us," and he smiled.

Would you recommend any of our resources in particular that helped you, Génesis?

I recommend all of your resources. Begin with *How God Can and Will Restore Your Marriage* and study *A Wise Woman* to prepare for married life when you're husband is home. Reading and studying the *By the Word of Their Testimonies* helped me see what these women did and to make sure I did the same. Each day, I did at least one lesson of your online courses, and I never missed starting my day with the Encourager.

Would you be interested in helping encourage other women, Génesis?

Yes, this is my calling.

Either way, Génesis, what kind of encouragement would you like to leave women with, in conclusion?

Above all things, God loves us. He wants us, more than anything, and is always ready to help us when we call on Him to take over. I know there are still a lot of things ahead on my journey of being restored, but God raised me up, gave me strength, dried my tears and told me "I want you to remain steadfast in your pursuit of my love and wisdom to help other women. I want to make you an instrument to guide the women of this generation to see the dangerous road they are traveling on. I've tested you, because I love you. Now that you understand that having only One Lover will complete you, you are ready to reach the hurting."

Darling, Heavenly Husband, You are the reason for my living!

Chapter 4

Adrianna

"And the peace of God, which surpasses
all comprehension, will guard your
hearts and your minds in Christ Jesus."
—Philippians 4:7

"Two Pastors Told Me
I had Grounds for Divorce"

Adrianna, how did your restoration actually begin?

My husband left me in May, shortly after we completed 10 years of marriage. We were arguing a lot and hurting each other with hateful and spiteful words. I had no wisdom, and so I argued. I was contentious and impertinent, and I began to suspect that there was another woman. After our argument, he left and said he was going to spend the day at his parents' house. When he came back that night, he said that he would be living with his parents and began to pack his things.

The months that followed were filled with so much anguish and pain. Not only did he just up and leave, he never contacted me, not once in several months. I heard from many people how he had a lot of hatred towards me and, due to not wanting to see me, he hardly saw our daughters and seemed not to care about them. About this same time, he left the church, started drinking and going out every night after work. Even though I suspected he was involved with another woman and told him I "knew" he was, in fact, he wasn't. Sadly, once gone and living a life of a single, he found (and began telling everyone about) his new girlfriend.

In my despair, I felt helpless and hopeless. I always believed that our marriage was forever and knew that God did not want separation or divorce. But, unfortunately, I did not receive good advice, even from pastors. I did everything wrong; I was full of doubts, and there was no one to help me with the answers I needed. I looked to God and asked

Him to speak to me, to help me. I contemplated filing for divorce, after two pastors told me I had grounds and God had someone else for me. But I did not know if it was right or wrong to do.

How did God change your situation, Adrianna, as you sought Him wholeheartedly?

After much searching for help and not getting anything that felt right to me, I went searching the Internet for help. I began researching about witchcraft, because I always believed that we were victims of things done to us and wanted the spell to be cast out. It was then that I found a site where someone was talking about the book *How God Can and Will Restore Your Marriage*, and then I found and came to RMI, and my whole world changed.

I started to read each one of your books, and slowly my behavior began to change, just because I was being fed the truth for the first time in my life. I no longer acted out with hatred, always arguing with everyone. I had an inner "peace that surpassed all understanding." I did not chase after my EH anymore. I'd been harassing him by phone, because of the money he was supposed to give me for our children. Once I started taking the course, pouring my heart out into my journals, that's when the real changes began to happen. I also read the daily praise reports in the Encourager, because I was filled with faith and hope on a daily basis.

My focus began to change from the negative to the positive. I woke up to seek God and worship Him with all my heart and spent precious moments with my Beloved Heavenly Husband. He cleansed my heart and took away all hatred towards everyone. When my husband showed up, I treated him with respect and affection, and I did not mention the money anymore. And this is when he started to come around, more and more often.

What principles, from God's Word (or through our resources), Adrianna, did the Lord teach you during this trial?

I learned to shut up, not to argue about anything, ever, and let it go. The courses helped me a lot. It seemed that every daily devotion and testimony were the answers I needed on that day, at every ordeal. God had a word for me. Many times, He used Erin's videos that seemed to answer my doubts at that very moment.

I have not finished reading the books I bought, because I found that I got more from the courses. If I missed a single day, I'd immediately find myself slipping back to my old ways. I had to repeat course 1 and 2, twice, before I took course 3, which was paramount to being ready for my husband's return (which happened faster than I'd imagine it would happen). Each of the courses, Erin's courses, and her words were the most important for my changing from the inside out, as she says.

What were the most difficult times that God helped you through, Adrianna?

It was when my EH often came to me for intimacy but was still living his single life. I knew that he had a girlfriend, and he was going to meet her, when he'd get up afterward. It bothered me, because everything was comfortable for him, having two of us. And, I confess, there came a time when I could not bear to be intimate with him, but I did it in obedience to the Lord. I thank God for my new relationship with my HH, or I wouldn't have been able to bear it. It was what He used to really help me fall in love with Him, which I asked Him to help me do—to be lovesick as Erin says she is.

Adrianna, what was the "turning point" of your restoration?

It was when I told the Lord that He was all I wanted and all I needed. I fell completely in love with my HH, and I no longer wanted my EH or my restoration anymore. My EH could instantly tell, and he thought I was interested in someone else.

Tell us HOW it happened, Adrianna. Did your husband just walk in the front door? Adrianna, did you suspect or could you tell you were close to being restored?

It happened when he noticed my disinterest, and I was apparently involved and in love with someone else. You can't fake this, because I tried more than once, when I read testimonies saying that's what led to their restoration. But until it's real, it just won't result in anything good.

Once I was entirely committed and in love with my HH, just as Erin says will happen, my EH was desperate to be with me. He called me and said he was coming home, said he was very homesick. When he arrived, he told me that he had read his Bible that morning, which he had not done since he left home, and he asked me if I wanted him to come back home to live as husband and wife. Could I forgive him? That same day, he broke up with OW and began asking me who I was involved with. I began to smile, and then told him.

Would you recommend any of our resources in particular that helped you, Adrianna?

I think all the materials are excellent. The book How God Can and Will Restore Your Marriage was the beginning of my journey, as well as A Wise Woman, to get ready for your husband coming home. And as I said, it was when I took your courses that I really began to see changes in me and in our relationship. The resources I used most, and still use, are Erin's My Beloved devotional, Encourager, and Be Encouraged eVideos.

Would you be interested in helping encourage other women, Adrianna?

Yes

Either way, Adrianna, what kind of encouragement would you like to leave women with, in conclusion?

Never give up. God is powerful and can do the impossible. Everything He does, when it's left to Him, is much more abundantly beyond what we ask or think. I had no idea how different my life would become due to this journey I began with Him.

Chapter 5

Doreen

"You have turned my mourning
into joyful dancing.
You have taken away my clothes
of mourning and clothed me with joy"
—Psalm 30:11

"Slowly and Methodically Killing Him"

Doreen, how did your restoration actually begin?

It all started during our 6th year of marriage. We were still childless and had a long history of many discussions, and in all of them, I was very disrespectful toward my husband. I didn't just speak the words, I shouted and humiliated him. My husband was always having to humble himself to make me happy and to avoid more fights with me.

In three or four "discussions," I ended them by stating that we'd be better off if we just got a divorce. The last time, I created a huge scene when I walked over to his car, dangling his keys, and threatened to leave him for good. As you can imagine, it wasn't a surprise when my husband told me that I was slowly and methodically killing him. Like most women's testimonies, I didn't even realize I was destroying my own marriage—tearing my life down with my own hands.

How did God change your situation, Doreen, as you sought Him wholeheartedly?

I had already realized that I was acting totally wrongly, but I thought I needed to change to please my husband, so that he would "love me" again and we'd be all right. Even though I've been a Christian since I was a child, I now knew God for the first time and realized I needed a Savior, but He wasn't yet my Lord, nor the Husband I needed. Not yet.

As I began to look for alternatives to "keeping" my husband with me, I stumbled onto the RMI website and found myself as a "less than a

Godly woman," not living as a Christian wife should, and I discovered just how wrong I'd been all these years. I proceeded to follow the journey set before me, purchasing resources, being spiritually fed daily with Encourager, and I started doing the courses. I began to seek God with a deep intensity, to become "precious in His sight" (1 Peter 3:2)! It was my Heavenly Husband who taught me to surrender all the cares of my life—indeed, my whole life—into His loving hands! "Delight yourself in the Lord and He will give you the desires of your heart" (Psalm 37:4).

I started to rest, to lay down in the green pastures (Psalm 1). Rather than fighting, I realized I needed to win my husband without a word, then stand by and watch Him do it (Exodus 14:13). My life changed dramatically, as I rested totally in the Lord. As time went by, there were times I still felt some anxiety, but I knew that the Lord knew me and loved me—despite any of my shortcomings and weaknesses. I began to let go. I knew that He had not finished the good work that began in my new abundant life. I knew it would all happen at the appointed time, and I was more than willing to wait, as I was so happy and full of joy!

What principles, from God's Word (or through our resources), Doreen, did the Lord teach you during this trial?

The Lord taught me the principle of God's sovereignty, even over free will, which was a huge turning point for me!

"The king's heart is like channels of water in the hand of the LORD; He turns it wherever He wishes" (Proverbs 21:1).

"A man's heart plans his way, but the Lord directeth his steps" (Proverbs 16.9 KJV).

What were the most difficult times that God helped you through, Doreen?

There were so many times that were difficult. Not hearing that he loved me hurt; in fact, he said he didn't know what he felt for me anymore. He started calling me by my full name and not the pet names he used to use. But when I brought it to my HH, He began calling me the sweetest of names. We had our own love songs that made my heart soar. So very soon, things that were missing, the things that were painful, all turned to joyful times of dancing.

"He will wipe away every tear from their eyes, and death will not exist any more—or mourning, or crying, or pain, for the former things have ceased to exist" (Revelation 21:4).

"You have turned my mourning into joyful dancing. You have taken away my clothes of mourning and clothed me with joy" (Psalm 30:11).

Probably the darkest moment was when he decided to leave the house for a week, to try to figure out what he felt about me and staying in our marriage. I say, it would have been the hardest, but because it was the moment that I first felt the peace of the Lord, and it was the week I found my abundant life and my HH, I breezed through it, as I never imagined that I could. I only have fond memories of that week with Him.

Doreen, what was the "turning point" of your restoration?

The turning point was the week he left, that I mentioned above. It was while he sought God's will for his life, whether or not God wanted him to continue our marriage, and I, in turn, found my true Love. As he sought God, I asked God to do whatever was His best for us, what was best for my husband's life, even if it meant removing him from my life for good. I was at the most peaceful place in my life, so it was easy to tell God to just go ahead and do His will, not mine. At that point, I could easily wait for restoration, and it no longer mattered how much time I needed to travel along my restoration journey. I had the strength of the Lord, who was carrying me, and I loved it.

Tell us HOW it happened, Doreen. Did your husband just walk in the front door? Doreen, did you suspect or could you tell you were close to being restored?

My husband left home on a Monday night, saying that he would spend that week away and on the weekend we would get together to talk, and I agreed. When I had read (in the *Word of their Testimony books* that I had purchased) the testimonies of women saying that they no longer cared about restoration and that, as they were doing the lessons, something happened, I believed them, of course. But never in a million years did I think it would ever happen to me, nor did I believe that I would no longer worry or care about anything, but it happened just like that!

By Wednesday, I felt peace that was unexplainable and woke up each morning to do the next day's lesson with joy, and I submitted one praise

report after another. As I praised God in my lesson, my husband called
me; Glory to God, I was shocked! He asked if we could have lunch
together the next day, which was a holiday. He said we needed to talk,
because he'd come to a decision. He was somber, but because I had
nothing to lose—since I had a Lover, I had my HH—I agreed to meet
and was excited no matter the outcome.

When we talked, he simply said that God had spoken to him and that
he'd failed as my spiritual leader. I nodded and later told him how much
I'd been praying for him to be my spiritual leader! He leaned over the
table and kissed me, and then I noticed his eyes tearing up.

As of today, we've been together for a little over five months! Praise
the Lord! I began writing my testimony a little over two weeks after he
came back, but I just couldn't send it. After our talk, even though he'd
come back, he came back not the way I wanted, nowhere near the
spiritual leader he'd promised to be. So I just figured it wasn't
restoration, yet.

In fact, after he returned, it was I who failed a lot, not him, because I
have not been gentle or quiet. My contentiousness returned, because
my relationship with my HH began to diminish, and I stopped traveling
along my RMI journey. Having my husband at home, working, and
going back to church (because that's the one way he had kept his
promise—when we began attending church together on Sundays), all
of this took up all my time. I stopped following the lessons completely;
I left off fasting for a while, because he was home, because he did not
agree with fasting (and prior to his return I was fasting 3 days a week).

Anyway, I stupidly began trying to "please my husband" again, above
anyone else, to my shame. Almost 3 months later, I just about lost my
restoration entirely! To finish me off, the enemy tempted me to snoop
and listen to gossip, and so I discovered things about the possibility of
an OW. Just as the contentious woman I had been (because I was on
this slippery slope gaining momentum), I confronted him. He confessed
that nothing happened physically, but his heart was torn. Thankfully,
this was the wakeup call I needed.

I'm so ashamed of my backsliding away from where I'd come in my
journey as His bride, but the Lord used this to call me back. I realized
that failing to give God the praise and holding out for a better testimony
was foolish. I do not want to go back to the old me, to my old life. I
want to go forward.

My husband and I are together, married, but I still long for a child. I believe the biggest trap is that my restoration is not happening the way I wanted it to. Instead of continuing my journey, I went back to the way I was living, the way that led me to this place of needing restoration. Instead of just asking Him how I could continue to fast, how I could steal away moments to be alone with my Lover, I totally turned my back on Him.

I know that God will complete the work He started in me. So, all I need to do is get back on track, remain in the middle of the narrow road of my journey and fall in love with my Beloved again (which has already started to happen :). My trust is that my God, Who began a good work in my life, is faithful to complete it, and I will wait for it, as my HH's bride.

Would you recommend any of our resources in particular that helped you, Doreen?

Yes, I have already recommended *How God Can and Will Restore Your Marriage,* your courses, Be Encouraged videos, and the Daily Encouragement blog.

Would you be interested in helping encourage other women, Doreen?

Yes!

Either way, Doreen, what kind of encouragement would you like to leave women with, in conclusion?

Do not give up! I had already thought of giving up, and I recently thought about it again, but I want to say, "I have fought the good fight, I have finished the course, I have kept the faith . . ." (2 Timothy 4:7). It's not us who need to fight. He wants a bride with a gentle and quiet spirit. Let the Lord fight for us, while we keep our eyes on Him and our hearts toward just loving Him.

God wants the Lord to be first in our lives! So come on, delight in His love, because He will take care of us and give us the desires of our hearts!

Chapter 6

Katie

"I am the vine, you are the branches;
he who abides in Me and I in him,
he bears much fruit, for apart from Me
you can do nothing."
—John 15:5

"Healed, Healthy, Whole and RESTORED!!"

Katie, how did your restoration actually begin?

Thank you so much, my Heavenly Husband—I give you all the honor, Glory and Praise!

My restoration journey began the day my husband told me he no longer wanted to be married and that he didn't love me anymore. That day, my mother introduced me to RMI, and I started reading your books and just looking to God for help, and that's when I found my HH.

My husband came back, after being gone for just 6 weeks. It happened sooner than I expected. He was with another woman, but I didn't really "know" until he came back and confessed to his adultery. My Beloved turned my husband's heart back toward Him! In the waiting, I was so well taken care of by My Beloved; He met all of my needs. Now that my husband has been back for about two weeks, I have struggled. I struggled with time with My Beloved and even just the balance of meeting his needs and my children's needs. I've cried out to My Beloved constantly, because I feel like giving up—especially when I think of my husband's body being with another woman.

Thankfully, by discovering this amazing ministry on the day my husband told me that he no longer loved me, I was able to fully give myself to my HH with no reservations. I allowed Him to keep testing my heart, as much as He needed, so that I could be complete in Him, because I didn't know how incomplete I was—even before I knew my marriage was in trouble.

I want to encourage you ladies. Our Maker wants to meet our needs; He wants to pour into us for His glory, for the sake of others around us, including our husbands. The tests have become harder, now that I'm restored, but I just keep seeking His face, asking Him to guide me and fill me up. I recognize now that there is nothing I can do without Him. John 15:5: "I am the vine, you are the branches; he who abides in Me and I in him, he bears much fruit, for apart from Me you can do nothing."

How did God change your situation, Katie, as you sought Him wholeheartedly?

Once I was able to just look to God for restoration, I saw how He began moving in my husband's heart. He set divine appointments for my husband and filled him with conviction. That was all happening while I was just going to my HH to meet my every need. This included being a Father to my children—at that time I struggled with them. When I struggled with their behavior, I would just ask my Beloved, since He as their Father would help them behave, and He did!

What principles, from God's Word (or through our resources), Katie, did the Lord teach you during this trial?

He taught me that He is my Husband, that He protects me, rescues me, and that my sense of security should only come from Him. I learned that He, and only He, is able to meet our every need and that our husbands are a great bonus, but our HH should be our main source!

What were the most difficult times that God helped you through, Katie?

The nights were so hard for me. I do not like sleeping alone, just wondering what my husband was doing and if he was being unfaithful. I didn't learn of his adultery until he returned, although, of course, I had an idea, but I didn't confront him about it. I would just ask my Beloved that if He would just hug me and let me feel His love, that if I could just see His face, I could make it through anything. Proverbs 3:24 says, "When you lie down, you will not be afraid; when you lie down, your sleep will be sweet." My Beloved was always faithful, and I could always feel His perfect Love and Peace. He would always give me new promises, as I read His Word.

Katie, what was the "turning point" of your restoration?

The turning point is when I finally let go. That week, my husband went to see his sister out of state. She's a Believer and was always hopeful that God would restore our marriage. That is where God showed up! My husband confessed his sin to his family first, and they prayed for him. My husband said that is when he felt the presence of God for the first time in a long time. The same night that was happening several states away, I was at home praising and worshiping my Beloved. My HH told me that I should start praising Him and worshiping Him, as if my marriage had already been restored.

Tell us HOW it happened, Katie. Did your husband just walk in the front door? Katie, did you suspect or could you tell you were close to being restored?

The night I was praising my Beloved, I knew my husband was going to stop by the next day to see my kids, once he arrived from the airport, because he had let me know. But then he had told me he would stop by later in the afternoon. That morning, he texted me early and asked if he could come over, because he "wanted to talk." I wasn't sure what about, because I didn't want to get my hopes up and discover that he wanted a divorce, but I was ready after reading Facing Divorce Again.

I was surprised how quickly he rushed over and began confessing all of his sins. As he was pouring his heart out, I was filled with this supernatural peace! I wasn't upset or hurt—I just knew that my husband needed to feel our Father's unconditional love. My husband mentioned that the way I had been treating him, while he was gone and would come to visit the children, was truly demonstrating the love of God. I had won him without a word and with a gentle and quiet spirit. I am so thankful; the contentious woman is gone!

Did you suspect, or could you tell you were close to being restored?

I knew my husband's heart was softening towards me, because he was more friendly and would talk to me a little more. But I didn't think my restoration would happen so soon. My husband was gone for 6 weeks. My husband would contact me every day. It didn't feel like he was pursuing me, because he was just asking about bills, asking about the kids, but he would still try to contact me every day. I will say the most difficult part is him actually being home again.

Would you recommend any of our resources in particular that helped you, Katie?

How God Can and Will Restore Your Marriage, *Be encouraged videos*, Abundant Life courses Finding the Abundant Life and Living the Abundant Life, Psalms and Proverbs.

Do you have favorite Bible verses that you would like to pass on to women reading your Testimonies? Promises that He gave you?

2 Chronicles 20:17 NLT
"You will not have to fight this battle. Take up your positions; stand firm and see the deliverance the Lord will give you, Judah and Jerusalem. Do not be afraid; do not be discouraged. Go out to face them tomorrow, and the Lord will be with you.'"

Proverbs 16:1 NLT
"We can make our own plans, but the Lord gives the right answer.

Isaiah 54:4-6 NLT
"Fear not; you will no longer live in shame.
Don't be afraid; there is no more disgrace for you.
You will no longer remember the shame of your youth
and the sorrows of widowhood.
For your Creator will be your husband;
the Lord of Heaven's Armies is his name!
He is your Redeemer, the Holy One of Israel,
the God of all the earth.
For the Lord has called you back from your grief—
as though you were a young wife abandoned by her husband,"
says your God.

Would you be interested in helping encourage other women, Katie?

Yes

Either way, Katie, what kind of encouragement would you like to leave women with, in conclusion?

Your HH is waiting for you to run to Him! He wants to meet your every need! He loves you more than words can express. He has chosen YOU for this, because he wants you closer to Him.

Chapter 7

Evangeline

"The wise woman builds her house,
But the foolish tears it down with her own hands."
—Proverbs 14:1

"Trying to be A Wise Woman"

Evangeline, how did your restoration actually begin?

Well, my marriage began to unravel because of the continuous fights I was having with my husband. We'd argue, because he was always late coming home. Then I'd get angry, because he spent all his time on his cell phone and ignored me when he was home. Almost every day was a hassle, and this was taking a toll on our marriage.

Then one day, the day of my birthday, we had a huge fight, because he came late to my party. I kept calling to find out where he was, and then when he arrived, I started complaining in front of everyone. He came back at me by saying he'd been thinking of moving in with his dad, which made me very angry, and I lost all reason—I said that if this is how he felt, then leave and don't bother to come home anymore. I told him to leave my party, pack his clothes and get out.

Even after he left, I still thought he would come back, because it was my birthday, but he did not come back; he didn't even call me. When it sunk in what I'd done, I was devastated.

How did God change your situation, Evangeline, as you sought Him wholeheartedly?

The first thing God showed me was that we cannot resolve things by speaking. Instead, we should keep our mouths closed and speak to the One who can calm us and take care of things that bother us. If there is a battle, it's our Husband's, and we are to stay by to watch. "You need not fight in this battle; station yourselves, stand and see the salvation of the Lord on your behalf . . . Do not fear or be dismayed . . . the Lord is with you" (2 Chronicles 20:17).

What principles, from God's Word (or through our resources), Evangeline, did the Lord teach you during this trial?

I learned to wait for the appointed time that God has for everything. I am very anxious by nature, so it took fasting and reading verses on waiting, over and over again, in order to change. I have learned a lot— so much I never knew. I began to ask God every day to give me wisdom, the patience to wait, and for His love to flow over me to bring me joy.

What were the most difficult times that God helped you through, Evangeline?

The hardest moment was when my husband said he did not love me anymore, that he needed some time to see if he was going to miss me and still want to be married. He said that our marriage was no longer what he'd expected, that he wanted to live separate lives. This was the worst time, because I also felt that our love had also been lost. But rather than give up, I wanted my husband with me. So, I went to my church for help. I wanted to know what to do, and they suggested divorce. Because I am a new believer, I wondered if this could be what we should do when a husband leaves us and wants to be separated, because I had my doubts. That's when I found your site and knew this wasn't the answer. God can and will restore.

Evangeline, what was the "turning point" of your restoration?

The turning point was when I began to seek God for the answers to everything that was happening in my life. I knew that going to anyone else would lead me to the pit of destruction. Also, it was the moment I knew that only God can turn the heart of my husband, no matter what his plans, and that God is in control. The spiritual battle is great, so I knew I needed to have a lot of wisdom to deal with many situations, which I found in *A Wise Woman,* so many things that are not taught anywhere else.

Tell us HOW it happened, Evangeline. Did your husband just walk in the front door? Evangeline, did you suspect or could you tell you were close to being restored?

We started talking to each other, the more I obtained a gentle and quiet spirit and never contacted him. He called one day, saying he was very discouraged because of the problems he was having at work. He also said that there were so many bills to pay, and his salary had been cut.

And, even then, they delayed paying him every month. So, anyway, several things began happening in his life.

He said he called because I was giving him strength, and that's when I said it wasn't my strength, and I began to share about the book I was reading, *A Wise Woman*. I shared my relationship with my HH, and I shared with him how He's who helped me find the way and find the strength to go through all the difficulties I'd recently faced. The more we spoke, the more I saw that God was beginning to soften his heart towards me — but mainly toward wanting to hear more about God and the relationship that I told him kept me calm and at peace.

He seemed to be taking it all in, but then suddenly he said he still did not know what to do with his life moving forward. This, I sensed, was the opportunity I'd ask God to give me. So I apologized for the way I treated him throughout our marriage and especially on my birthday. I asked him to forgive me, and he said, yes, he would. He said he wanted to come home, but didn't know for sure if I'd changed. Later, he came home with his clothes and never left.

Though we are restored, we are living one day at a time. I am trying to be a *Wise Woman*, and he is also studying his *Wise Man*. I am being more affectionate, more understanding, and I am always asking God when I have any question. When I need love, I don't run to my husband and demand or seduce him like before. Instead, I go to the source of my love, my Heavenly Husband, and what's so surprising is that soon afterward my husband began coming to me to be more affectionate.

We are even making plans to build our home. Even in this, I've given it to God. My HH fulfills all my dreams, takes care of all my concerns, and only God will make it happen, if it is His will. Even though I came to a place in my relationship with my HH that I no longer needed to hear it, the day came when my EH said he still loved me so much that, even when he thought of separation, he really didn't want it, and that the moment I said I was wrong, he realized that he loved me and always had. I am so in awe of God and how amazingly He works in our lives. God is wonderful; never doubt that when we think that there is no way, He comes to change everything and give us everything.

Would you recommend any of our resources in particular that helped you, Evangeline?

Yes. Of course, I recommend *A Wise Woman*. I know everyone recommends *How God Can and Will Restore Your Marriage*, which also helped me a lot, especially in that difficult period when I started to look for more help on the internet. I searched looking for restored marriage testimonies, and that's when I found the RMI. I liked the Restore Your Marriage a lot; it speaks of everything that really happens in our marriages, our mistakes, anyway... I have not finished reading it, because I keep coming back to *A Wise Woman*. This is the book that I read first, which helped me so much and got my life on the right course, and it's what I know will help me stay on course throughout my life. It's not just about how to get a husband back, but also how to live as a woman, not just a wife.

Would you be interested in helping encourage other women, Evangeline?

Yes

Either way, Evangeline, what kind of encouragement would you like to leave women with, in conclusion?

To everyone, I say, do not to give up or be discouraged by any circumstances. We have to believe that God has the best waiting for us. If we are obedient, repent of our mistakes and seek Him with all our heart, He will hear us and send us the help at just the right time.

Chapter 8

Alma

"I waited patiently for the Lord;
and He inclined to me and heard my cry."
—Psalm 40:1

"I was Going Crazy Becoming Suicidal"

Alma, how did your restoration actually begin?

It all started when my EH "earthly husband" started his new job. We had just been blessed with our baby daughter, and he felt the need to work harder as expenses increased. I never accepted this job very much, because I knew that he would not have a fixed schedule and that he would have to travel a lot, eventually leaving us alone. So after some time, he ended up moving away from me emotionally, becoming cold and distant. I asked him about it, during some of our conversations, but he never said much.

It was due to this emotional distance that he fell in love with someone else—a woman who worked with him. I was always very contentious, demanding, and I started to accuse him (when nothing was really happening), which just made him go ahead and find someone. I know that when this all began (when I first began accusing him) that nothing had happened yet, but due to my attitudes and the many weaknesses within our marriage, the enemy found the crack and began to try to destroy my family.

We also stopped attending church as a family. More often I'd go, but I left my husband home on his own. We both felt that everything was under control. We believed that it was no longer necessary to seek God, because we had a beautiful daughter; I was taking university courses; I wanted to further my education, and he had the dream job.

Then it all fell apart. He got involved with OW, and I started to panic. In one of our many discussions, I even said that I would take my life and our daughter's life, if he made the choices for himself, so that he could go on and live happily without us. I was so foolish; instead of seeking help from God, I wanted to prove to my family that his cheating was the reason why I was going crazy and becoming suicidal.

Then a few months later, he left home, and I became horribly depressed—to the point that my parents feared I (or he) would do something to hurt me and our daughter. When he left home, he said nothing to me, but I knew he left and was living with OW. But he just left; he didn't divorce me. He just left and disappeared for several days.

It was a month after he left that I felt God calling me to fight for our marriage, and I was directed to the RMI website, where I did find Hope at Last. I confess that I was not a good student, because I read the lessons, but I did not apply them. I never journaled, so I never got to the point of the principles sinking in. But I learned from the pain to start journaling, which helped me apply what I learned into my everyday life. Now, when I realize I'm failing, I know it's because I haven't journaled.

And so my journey of restoration began, in the midst of intense pain, utter despair and buckets of crying.

How did God change your situation, Alma, as you sought Him wholeheartedly?

Beloved, in the beginning, I fought hard against this restoration journey. I always told my EH that if there was ever unfaithfulness on his part, we were over, and I would divorce him. But God broke me of all that pride. He called me to distance myself from everyone. Most days, I was alone in my prayer room, and there God showed me that divorce was not His plan for my family. He had to get me out of my comfortable surroundings, out of my normal life, to search for Him all the time and renew my mind with His Word.

What principles, from God's Word (or through our resources), Alma, did the Lord teach you during this trial?

I learned the principle of letting go, of winning without words, of waiting patiently for the Lord. At every moment since the beginning of this journey, His Word is the only word that matters. As in Psalm 40:1, "I waited patiently for the Lord; and He inclined to me and heard my cry."

What were the most difficult times that God helped you through, Alma?

The most difficult time I spent was watching my daughter look for her father and not find him. She saw her cousins with their parents, and hers wasn't around. The other difficulty was the principle of letting go, handing everything over to Him. As humans, we always want to take a little action, but when we do, we lose our blessing.

Another really difficult time He helped me through was leaving my home, then having to go through living with my mother-in-law, and then living with my parents. That was very difficult, because I wanted my independence; I wanted to raise my daughter on my own.

Another thing I always said when I was younger, and I wasn't yet married, is that I would be totally independent—how silly I was! I ended up living everything I said I would never do.

Alma, what was the "turning point" of your restoration?

The turning point was when I really, truly let go, because the Lord became my HH "Heavenly Husband." Once He was truly first, I started to be happy. Everything I wanted or needed I simply had to ask it of Him, and He would move mountains on my behalf. He'd turn the tide, and I watched, as He started using all the difficult circumstances to my favor. I started to choose Him over everyone and anything—and this is when I really began to live life. Day after day, believing only in His Word, His love gave me the abundant life that is worth living.

"'For the Lord has called you, like a wife forsaken and grieved in spirit, even like a wife of one's youth when she is rejected,' says your God" (Isaiah 54:6).

Tell us HOW it happened, Alma. Did your husband just walk in the front door? Alma, did you suspect or could you tell you were close to being restored?

Once I was His bride, my EH began to come to visit our daughter, and I'd go to spend time walking in the park, which made him feel free to play with her (and long for me). While in our home, he began doing things that needed fixing or taking out the trash, things he used to do when he was living with us.

There were days when I'd arrive back home from my walking time with my Lover that I noticed my EH appeared disturbed, lost and sad. I always asked my Beloved that He would open his eyes for my EH to see that he needed to have what I had. About six months after he'd moved out, he arrived to spend time with our daughter but instead asked if he could go with me on my walk. I explained that it was my time to be alone, that it was a relationship with the Lord that had changed me, but that he could meet me at the park's play area.

It was there that he told me of his regrets and how much he tried to find a way to fix everything. I said there was nothing to fix, just come home if you want. Then I said, if you don't want to come home, it was fine with me, because I am so happy with my life. He said, "I want to be happy like you are." The next weekend, he moved back home.

Would you recommend any of our resources in particular that helped you, Alma?

Yes, all of them, every book and course you offer. The books, *How God Can and Will Restore Your Marriage* and *A Wise Woman*, both laid the foundation for my restoration. Journaling through all the Abundant Life courses, beginning with Finding the Abundant Life, is what I recommend.

I also recommend the Daily Encourager, devotionals, and not forgetting the Bible as our main source. Every one of your resources has a vital message for wives seeking restoration. Each lesson should be gone through in its own time, and sometimes you will need to return to redo them again, and again and again.

Would you be interested in helping encourage other women, Alma?

Yes

Either way, Alma, what kind of encouragement would you like to leave women with, in conclusion?

Do not give up on what God has promised you. Your HH will be with you at all times, even the most difficult, if you put Him first. Never trade Him for temporary pleasures of this earth.

Chapter 9

Kristy

"And I will give you a new heart,
and a new spirit I will put within you.
and I will remove the heart of stone from your
flesh and give you a heart of flesh."
—Ezekiel 36:26

"Brought Me Low to Have Me All to Himself"

Kristy, how did your restoration actually begin?

My EH decided to leave but came back a month later, but left again 8 months later. We were fighting, and there had been infidelity by both parties. I was devastated, and I was a part of a standers' ministry for one year, before praying for my eyes to be opened. I came across this ministry on Google. My EH had up a huge hate wall. I was very contentious, manipulative, demanding and bossy. I had demanded attention, and I would not stand for anything less. He was fed up, packed his bags and moved in with a coworker, who was the OW.

I was at my lowest and thought that there could be no hope for my marriage, since it was my second marriage. Every other Christian marriage ministry said that my marriage could not be saved, because I was committing adultery. I had been praying for a sign that the Lord actually wanted to restore my marriage, and was about to give up, but then I came across your website while searching...but the funny thing was that I had searched many times before and had never come across this website.

When I first came, I confessed in my third journal that I was still angry with my EH and the OW. But I said, "I want the anger and bitterness to be removed from my heart, and I want to see them as God sees them." I prayed in my journal, "Lord, thank you for bringing me this far on the journey. It feels so long, and yet when I read other people's testimonies, I feel guilty for ever complaining about my situation. Please change me to be a loving wife and woman and to be able to see my EH and the OW through your eyes."

I also prayed, "Lord, turn my heart completely to you and heal my broken heart. I desire you to be my everything...remove my desire for my earthly husband, and let me let go of him completely. I can't do it alone, Lord. I need you."

How did God change your situation, Kristy, as you sought Him wholeheartedly?

He broke me. I fasted a lot and got rid of cable and Facebook. I took long walks. He drew me to Him. The pain was more than I could bear, but it became a little easier daily. He turned me into a submissive wife, but then I became almost too quiet, and my EH was very skeptical of the changes.

After filling out my MEQ, the next thing I did was to become a partner and began giving 10% of my income as an offering. I didn't let go of my church until later on in my journey.

Write a "Letter to the Lord."

Lord, change me to be a woman that is after you and only you. I am desperate to have all of your love. Lead me to people that you want to be brought into my life. Show me how to be the woman you want me to be.

What would you say to His newer brides to Encourage them in regard to what you LEARNED?

Dear Brides, I'm right back at the beginning again, and I feel like I've failed, but after reading more, I realize He brought me low to have me all to Himself. Surrender your heart to Him. He loves us all so much.

What would you say to ENCOURAGE women to READ our books?

These books are uplifting and they help you get through the darkest hours.

Continue to ask God to change you. It is very, very painful, but there is a plan. Even though we don't understand it, He is lining everything up in perfect sequence to fall into place at the right time.

Yes, people have said I have become very quiet. Often they ask what is wrong, because I am usually a very people person. I just don't have anything to talk about anymore, because I realize I was a gossip, and a lot of my relationships were built on slandering others. It is so sad and makes me want to tell others: please do not fall into that pit.

What principles, from God's Word (or through our resources), Kristy, did the Lord teach you during this trial?

Let go, and stop snooping. Stop being demanding or making ultimatums. Let my Lord make the changes in my everyday life and with my EH.

I also began tithing to my storehouse, after signing up to be a partner— which was the second form I submitted after my marriage evaluation questionnaire. I just knew that verse in Malachi was true, and I stayed faithful all these years—seeing just how faithful He has been to His Word.

What were the most difficult times that God helped you through, Kristy?

Most difficult was knowing that my EH was with the OW and that she was everything he ever wanted. I also spent all my holidays alone.

Kristy, what was the "turning point" of your restoration?

Things turned when I stopped pursuing my EH, let go of my church and started focusing on other things in life (Jesus, my family, and others). The hate wall came down. We started out as friends...we started doing things together, and it has taken 5 years to become somewhat close again.

Tell us HOW it happened, Kristy. Did your husband just walk in the front door? Kristy, did you suspect or could you tell you were close to being restored?

At times, I would think something was about to happen, but after 5 years, I honestly was close to giving up and accepting I was to remain alone. As of today, I still am not sure if I want to live together, but I never want to take for granted what the Lord has done, and I repent often to even have such a negative thought.

Tell us HOW it happened? Did your husband just walk in the front door?

No. My lease was coming to an end, and my EH asked me what I thought about moving in with him to save money and to finish remodeling his home. At this moment, he has told me he is not in love with me, is afraid for the future and is not sure we can last, but he thinks it is financially beneficial. I praise God, because even though it is not the fairy tale I was dreaming of, God is opening the door, and I know He will take care of the rest.

Would you recommend any of our resources in particular that helped you, Kristy?

Every single thing that can be offered through this ministry!

Trust in the Lord with all your heart, and lean not on your own understanding;

How God Can and Will Restore Your Marriage also *A Wise Woman.* All of the *By the Word of Their Testimonies,* and going through online courses. Daily Encourager, HH, the Abundant Life courses Finding the Abundant Life, and HopeAtLast.com .

Would you be interested in helping encourage other women, Kristy?

Yes. I don't have an encouragement partner, but I kept a journal, since my phone was too small to turn in reports.

Either way, Kristy, what kind of encouragement would you like to leave women with, in conclusion?

Don't ever give up. Never take for granted any small or big miracle from the Lord. He is in control of everything—right down to the hair on our heads.

Dear Brides,

I know many of you do not feel this love for the Lord that so many women talk about, but I believe if we stick to it, make a commitment and lean in to our Lord, we will all find the abundant life that so many of these women talk about.

Chapter 10

Lori

"O LORD my God, I cried to You for help,
and You healed me."
—Psalm 30:2

"Pregnant, Alone, Full of Self-Pity"

Lori, how did your restoration actually begin?

Hello everyone, I'm so excited to let you know the good news—my marriage has been restored!! My husband and I have reconciled, living as husband and wife for a few months after experiencing turmoil in our marriage (as the result of adultery).

It all started when I got pregnant, and that's when so many arguments led me to mistrusting my husband, which led to him distancing himself from me. He was finishing his doctorate degree in a nearby city, practically living there (staying the night on the couch of a friend when he'd study too late to drive home). Which, of course, contributed to our distance emotionally, and his being gone led to an open invitation for the enemy to get a foothold—when he became involved with a fellow classmate.

Thankfully, I didn't have to find out myself or from someone telling me of his unfaithfulness. He came to me and confessed what he did and asked for forgiveness, crying so hard it broke my heart.

Unfortunately, it did not take long for everything to change. Soon after forgiving him, I began accusing him of cheating, and all too soon, he changed his mind, because I was far from a gentle and quiet spirit. So, he again came to me, said he loved me, but we could not be together anymore. Since he already lived in another city, and it was normal for him to be gone, our separation was not noticeable by any of our friends or family.

Sadly, I lost my footing, I fought in my own strength, and soon I asked for help from our church's pastor. He helped by way of prayer, but had little experience on the subject of marriage restoration, at least not in the way I needed. Instead, like so many restored marriage testimonies I studied to help me along my journey, he suggested singles groups telling me that God might have someone better for me! "Rubbish!!" I yelled at him, and I began searching for another church that believed in restoration, but I didn't find one, not one.

How did God change your situation, Lori, as you sought Him wholeheartedly?

Seeking God led me to search for "marriage restoration" on the internet, looking for marriages that had been restored. I ended up reading some reviews about the book *How God Can and Will Restore Your Marriage,* which helped me a lot. In a very interesting turn of events, I could not get access to the whole book, just the first chapter.

I later understood that the Lord first wanted to heal me, so I began to spend my time praying and crying out to the Lord to help me genuinely forgive my husband and the other woman, and God faithfully healed the intense deep wounds that had been caused by adultery. He healed this pain, which was almost unbearable, pain I did not want to feel anymore, which had often festered. This pain only passed when I locked myself in the bedroom and cried at the feet of My Beloved, facedown on the carpet. He alone, and no one else, understood me. He alone knew the pain I felt, because He had felt it too—from what He'd gone through when He was betrayed. He alone calmed me down and often made me sleep in peace.

"The Lord is my Shepherd, I shall not want. He makes me lie down in green pastures; He leads me beside quiet waters. He restores my soul" (Psalm 23: 1-3).

What is more interesting is that the Lord had been dealing with me about "letting go" and trusting Him, without me having any idea how to do it. This was confirmed when I finally was given access to the entire book and took course 1. It was not easy to apply this principle, but I confess I was relieved to know that I did not need to pursue my EH and did not need to know anything of what he did. Of course, it was My Beloved guarding me all the time, without me even knowing the principles so wisely taught here!!

What principles, from God's Word (or through our resources), Lori, did the Lord teach you during this trial?

All the principles were in some way important to help me along my journey, but "letting go" was the key, as every other restored marriage testimonies I studied said, too. I had never heard of this principle in such depth as I learned here, but I saw the destruction of so many women who tried to get me to read and/or join one of the Covenant or Standers groups—who actually encourage you to pursue rather than letting go of a wayward husband. The rejection and pain is awful, but worse is how it feeds the flesh, missing the reason why He's called us to travel this journey. This crisis happened so that we could experience Him as our HH and gain the gentle and quiet spirit that is precious to God.

What were the most difficult times that God helped you through, Lori?

The most difficult times were during my pregnancy, due to being alone and full of self-pity. It was also difficult after my daughter was born, as she was very sensitive to my moods, and she cried all the tim— whenever I failed to remain calm and surrounded by the love of my Heavenly Husband.

After I had my daughter and realized that my emotions were dictating her mood, I sought the Lord, Who helped me to go through everything always holding His hand, or He'd carry me, forever strengthening and guiding me.

Lori, what was the "turning point" of your restoration?

The turning point in my restoration happened soon after I arrived from a foolish, silly plan I made. I drove to where my EH lived, with the purpose of convincing him to return home. I was leaving my peaceful shelter where my HH was with me, and my daughter was only one week old. I fought the battle with my own weapons, following the advice of several pastors, who all told me to fight for what was rightfully mine; they said that this is how God would give me my miracle of restoration. You'd think I would have remembered what pastors think and believe, but I still was a silly woman. (2 Timothy 3:6-7), "For among them are those who enter into households and captivate silly women weighed down with various impulses, always learning and never able to come to the knowledge of Truth."

Oh, how wrong they were! God will do His part, but only when we are willing to give it all to Him! The Bible says to stand by and watch (Exodus 14:13). I was not following Him but instead had been following what someone else told me to do—something Erin warns us about. So, unfortunately, I did what the pastors directed me to do (which was totally contrary to what I learned here a few months later). I believed that, although it was a mistake, the Lord, with His infinite mercy, would grant me favor. But I confess that after what happened I was close to giving up, and I decided they were right—I needed to find someone new. I even joined a Christian dating site, after this blow to my faith.

It was this that got my attention. I never wanted any other man, and here I was doing something that's so not me! I realized how following the path of anyone who tells us to do something that's contrary to God's Word (which is why we must know it ourselves) is so horribly dangerous!!!

During this time, after almost falling into adultery myself, I found my faith increased, and He strengthened me as never before. Although I did what I "thought" was right, and in fact was not, I later turned to and relied deeply on the Lord, my HH, like never before. I watched how God used it for good (Romans 8:28), to show me just how easily I could have fallen into adultery myself, because my pastors were not His sheep but men clothed in wolves' skin.

After this I sought the Lord more, spent more time studying the Abundant Life course, letting go of marriage restoration entirely (because God said He would restore so I didn't need to bother with it), and because of this, my faith in God's ability to do it without any help from me increased.

It was during this time that I focused on helping other women, to do my part in producing some fruit of my own, sowing the seeds of Hope At Last, as others had done for me (when they offered me chapter 1 of RYM book), not really knowing I was being both an Evangelist and Minister.

Getting back to the turning point, brought on by my greatest mistake, the situation between my husband and I only got worse, because I stayed where he lived, unwilling to leave. He told me to leave, and I did not obey, but instead, I argued and tried to convince him of his madness. I took it all the way to even challenging him with my "self-righteousness," saying that God would act in my favor, because I was a righteous person.

Later, when I remembered the nonsense I was talking about, I was embarrassed and felt ashamed (thankfully my HH led me to read one of Erin's living lessons regarding guilt, so I could be set free from this). Anyway, my EH became even angrier, infuriated with me, and wanted more distance after this. It's crazy to think back that I stayed there in his room until I had not one more thing to say, and only then did I return back home to focus on my HH and take care of my newborn daughter.

Tell us HOW it happened, Lori. Did your husband just walk in the front door? Lori, did you suspect or could you tell you were close to being restored?

Despite coming home supposedly "defeated," I did not give up. I kept relying strongly on the Lord, and I began to hear Him speaking to my heart—that He would resolve that situation in His own way, in His appointed time, that it was no longer for me to worry about and that He was in control of EVERYTHING! Now I had really managed to give it all away (letting go, even though I did not know this principle very well, because, as I said at the beginning, at that time I still had no access to the book), to the point of saying in prayer that I did not care about my restoration anymore, because I did not need my husband to make me happy. My HH is who made me happier than I'd ever been in my life. I was cherished, looked after, and wanted for nothing.

Experiencing the valley of when I had searched and pursued my EH, saying to everyone "I could not live without him"—oh how wrong I was! In my Beloved Heavenly Husband's embrace is what really completed me. I simply loved how He loved me and made me feel like I was the most beloved and desired woman of all the earth. I just wanted Him and pleaded and wept desperately for Him, for more of Him in me; I did not want anyone else.

Shortly after I got to this point, I received news from my sister, who lived in the same city as my EH. She said she had seen my EH with the OW at the mall, and I stopped her before she shared the details. I told her I no longer wanted my husband, because I had met and fallen in love with another man. She was in shock, and after I explained it was my Beloved HH and how He made me feel, our conversation shifted to talking only about Him, and we hung up elated.

It was exactly two days after I said this when my EH began to text and call me. He left several text messages, and when I didn't reply, he called me several times. I did not answer, because when I saw his first text, I silenced my cell phone. It wasn't until after I nursed my daughter that I saw just how many times he tried to contact me.

The next day, he called me again, but this time I answered because my HH told me, "This is the appointed time, Lori." My EH began by asking about us, saying that he loved me, and asked if I loved him too. I hesitated, then finally whispered, "yes." There were several days of calls of this type; each time he said that he wanted to come home, that he could not stand being apart from me any longer. But I was so content in my relationship with my HH; I didn't care if it ever happened. I know my EH could sense this, which only heightened his desire for me (which Erin says will happen when we truly are His bride!)

Our restoration was complete, when he came home after receiving his doctorate and found a residency close by our home. Glory of God! My EH came back, when I no longer wanted it and least expected it (because we were told that there were no hospitals nearby accepting new residents to their program). Only God could do this!

Would you recommend any of our resources in particular that helped you, Lori?

I recommend all materials from your ministry, because each are precious and filled with the way we need to live—not only in our marriages but as a woman, mother, sister, friend, neighbor and coworker. As I said, I am especially devoted to the *How God Can and Will Restore Your Marriage* book, and I would never miss a morning reading the Daily Encourager.

Would you be interested in helping encourage other women, Lori?

I most certainly want to continue to reach out and minister to other women.

Either way, Lori, what kind of encouragement would you like to leave women with, in conclusion?

LOOK TO THE LORD!!!!!! Do not look at the circumstances. He promises to bring you through, so never give up on Him. Give up on trying to restore your marriage; only then will God take over and finish what He started. But first, He's working on you, and then He'll begin working on your EH. Everything is easier with HIM. Become His bride and find out for yourself!

Chapter 11

Wendy

"...may be able to comprehend with
all the saints what is the breadth and length
and height and depth, and to know the love of Christ
which surpasses knowledge, that you
may be filled up to all the fullness of God."
—Ephesians 3:18-19

"Adultery was Not Just on His Side"

Wendy, how did your restoration actually begin?

Fortunately, I found the RMI just three months after my husband left us on Christmas Eve. I believe I was guided by God to go on the Internet and search for restored marriages, which was my Divine Appointment. I'll never forget that day when I found hope.

At first, I just signed up to receive the Praise Reports, just something to feed my spiritual arrogance. I believed that I was in control of everything, until the end of March. Everything changed, after I'd been following another ministry and did everything they said was my right as his covenant wife. I dutifully and eagerly was chasing my husband, sending him texts and emails, showing up where I found out he'd be.

Due to my separation, my Visa had run out, so I had to return to my own country, to live with my parents with our daughter, while my husband stayed in the United States, where we had lived. After I was back for a few days, I got an email from him saying that, for him, everything was done and finished, and there was no chance we could resume having the kind of life we'd been living. I was in shock; I just never saw it coming.

How did God change your situation, Wendy, as you sought Him wholeheartedly?

God had my attention, so instead of just entertaining myself with praise reports, I began to read the book *How God Can and Will Restore Your Marriage* and *A Wise Woman*. As I read each page, He began to uncover my mistakes and sins, like peeling back the petals of an onion. During our marriage, there was adultery, not just on my husband's side, but I, too, had committed this sin and kept it hidden from him.

As I was reading each book for the third time, I started writing in both books, not just highlight portions. I started to write notes near each verse and principle, in the margin, every time my Lord showed me another sin and the mistakes I'd made during our marriage. I wrote, and each time I did, my heart broke. At the end of the book, with my heart totally broken, I drafted a single email to my EH asking for forgiveness for everything I had done in our marriage—each time I'd accused him, confronted him, for all my contentiousness, self-righteousness, and for being a "Pharisee." I asked him to forgive me for having complained about everything and for not respecting him as my husband.

Instead of getting a reply, several days went by, and he did not answer me, so I went back to my old ways and started chasing after him, and, of course, it only made things worse.

My husband's silence was another wake-up call for me. God made it clear that I had to rely on Him for everything. I read and studied the testimonies; that helped me a lot and got me to the point of realizing what was missing—having a relationship with the Lord. I began the first Abundant Life course, and, by the end, I got to the point of waking up thinking only of Him, which I had thought was impossible, and believe me—it is not! I never in a million years believed I could be someone who called herself His bride, and I want Him even more than I wanted my marriage restored or my husband back.

I changed the people I hung around; I changed the sort of clothes I wore, not just because it was something that my EH always said he wanted, but because I wasn't doing it for him anymore. I was doing it for my new Husband, and, for the first time, it was no longer about what I wanted. I became submissive to the Lord—doing things I did not do in marriage—knowing that the Lord was looking into my heart and pouring His love into me, made me different.

As my journey progressed, people at first believed I'd had a mental breakdown, but as time went by, they began to notice the change was more of a transformation. I became a very happy person, content, and aware of other people's needs, not just my own. I knew that I was reaching the place that God had for me all my life. I was becoming the servant, the friend, the woman, the mother and the wife (as His bride) that He had designed for me and that I did not know how to be, until He led me here.

What principles, from God's Word (or through our resources), Wendy, did the Lord teach you during this trial?

There were many principles that I learned. I am flabbergasted, because although we read the Bible as Christians, we think we can just live our lives, ignoring the Lord, never apply the principles in His Word, but it's not supposed to be like that!

Today, I read the Bible with a Concordance nearby, and when I encounter any negative feeling or thought, I quickly look up a verse, find the original word, look up more verses and then write it all down on my cards. For the first time, when I have an encounter "with my enem", I speak less, and I listen more and remain agreeable. I learned to have a meek and quiet spirit that is precious to the Lord, and, as He says, I have learned to be content during my Restoration Journey, whether it's on the mountain top or in the deepest of valleys.

Today I know that I can win my EH without words, and anything I need to know I can go to God to give me wisdom. Before I decide in any given situation, I stop and speak to Him to know what to do. And unbelievably and incredibly, each and every time the Lord "creates situations" to answer me and leads me along the correct path to take and to the decisions I should make.

"Letting go" is the most difficult, just like everyone says, and it is the most important for us to succeed in to complete the restoration journey. Now I understand letting go, this one act of the heart, shows our "FULL TRUST" in the Lord and in God's ability to restore our marriage.

Many things have changed in my life since beginning this journey. I constantly read the books and reread lessons, rather than entertaining myself by watching the telly or surfing through social media. Even after restoration, I continue to go back to renew principles (primarily in the Abundant Life books) to make certain I am not sliding down the slippery slope of putting my marriage or EH first. I must continue keeping Him in First place, remaining a work in progress, in order for this to succeed and to keep the blissful happiness I experienced as His bride. After restoration, as before, we all have to refresh ourselves in the principles we have learned here, for our own good, for our families and for those who are watching our lives.

What were the most difficult times that God helped you through, Wendy?

Without a doubt, the most difficult time that the Lord helped me through was to resist pursuing my EH. It felt so good in the flesh, and from associating with all the other standers, it was like coming off of drugs. There were many hours I was facedown on the floor praying, begging the Lord for help to forget my EH and to want only Him. I wanted with all my heart to keep my mind on the Lord and have Him the only person in my heart. I wanted to love Him as never before and to feel His transforming love to be all I wanted and all I needed.

I knew God needed to work on me, and I was not willing to back down. I simply didn't want to slip into my old ways, which is so easy to do. It finally happened, but it became very difficult once again, when we began to communicate and talk again. I did not know how to deal with the situation, of having him around, how I should speak and deal with having totally changed my way of communicating with him. But each time the Lord directed me, after much fasting and time in my prayer closet, just being alone with Him.

Today, I know that everything becomes easier and second nature, once we have a deep connecting with our HH, because all the direction comes from Him, as we naturally want to walk according to His will and not our own, free to flourish and no longer living a life that is so destructive and useless.

Wendy, what was the "turning point" of your restoration?

Without a doubt, it was when I let go, no doubt when I put Him first in my life and heart. Also, when I realized it was the salvation of my EH that was at stake, if I stayed living as I'd been. Also, when I was no longer fasting for the restoration of my marriage, nor for myself. One day, I woke up and decided to begin a 40-day fast, for his salvation and to have a genuine encounter with the Lord like never before. On the first day of fasting, in just one hour of praying for his salvation, he contacted me.

I want to remind each of you reading my testimony that as you are changing, being transformed, your spouse will also be. I never believed that was true, but it is. And it's done without a single word from you, due only to the change He's making inside of you, dear ones. So let it go; let God do it. Let God restore your marriage, as the book says.

Tell us HOW it happened, Wendy. Did your husband just walk in the front door? Wendy, did you suspect or could you tell you were close to being restored?

Yes, I suspected. The day before it happened, God had shown me in His Word (Isaiah 38:1-7 and 2 Kings 20:1-7) about when King Hezekiah receives a death sentence from the prophet and how he wept, and then he says, God will pardon him and give him more years.

In fact I had other signs, because the situation in my EH's life became very complicated professionally, after our separation, and with that his financial situation had been compromised; then I also noticed that God was talking to him about the restoration, because he told me he'd been thinking about it, but he was still resisting, due to his financial ruin. I believe he was embarrassed, yet at the same time, he did not want to lose contact with me. Let me assure everyone, this wasn't just because of my transformation, but because the closer I became with my HH, the more He was to me, the further away from my EH I stayed. I completely ignored him (and this was the state of my heart, not just my actions with the intent of faking letting go), which is when he first started sending me emails, asking me, then begging me to write back (because I would never reply to his emails).

I no longer looked for him; I did not ask anyone about him. It was he who wrote, pouring out his regrets. One email he sent included one of the prayers we were taught in one of Erin's books, in RYM, about praying the thorn fence around your husband, so he could not find his way. He said exactly what we pray: "I have come to the conclusion that I must return to you, because I have always wanted you from the beginning!" When I read that, I remembered the prayer I'd prayed (because I'd let go of praying for him or restoration), but He'd heard, set an appointed time (when I would want my HH more than anything), and He did it! Thank you, my precious Husband!

I learned to take all my promises about specific things to the Lord and speak His Word as my own. Doing this in my everyday life, I declared His promises over everyone. When the Lord gave me a Word about anything, I remained steadfast in it, until I saw the promise materialize.

With this, I learned a new faith, an effective and precious intimacy, and peace only increased. So when I was first asked to return to the United States, and then he pulled back and said no, I was at perfect peace, and I readily agreed it was for the best. Sure enough, the next I heard was to watch for my tickets to arrive, and we boarded the plane and were reunited at the same airport where I'd left, alone. I was a different person this time, and so was my husband.

Our HH makes everything perfect, and His word does not come back empty.

Would you recommend any of our resources in particular that helped you, Wendy?

I have and will recommend forever, not only during a crisis but for the maintenance of each and every marriage: *How God Can and Will Restore Your Marriage*, really studying *A Wise Woman* workbook, pouring out your heart in each lesson when taking the courses, review the videos, and—especially—reading through the Bible during your fasting.

Then to solidify it all, to find your HH, take the Abundant Life courses, beginning with Finding the Abundant Life, so you won't just find hope at last but love at last—love that lasts!

Would you be interested in helping encourage other women, Wendy?

Yes. Not only am I interested, I already have a group of 10 women that I meet with, where we share only praise. We discuss the many ways our HH cares for us throughout the week, and each of us leaves with our faces glowing! It also serves to keep Him first in my life, so that I do not fall into the trap or onto the slippery slope of focusing on my EH.

Either way, Wendy, what kind of encouragement would you like to leave women with, in conclusion?

I understand that "letting go" is what most women fear. Yet, you must believe in the Word of the Lord and put Him first. It's His love that will make all the changes in your life. We must focus on what God created us to be, and it's not just to get a husband back.

In addition, if God is demanding something from you, give it; do not hesitate; do not delay, because each time you do, you are only postponing your blessings from happening. Don't be like the people of

Egypt who stayed 40 years going around the same mountain. God has conditions to work in your life. At first, it will hurt, but His love is the healing balm that will soothe your soul and spirit, calming you of your addiction of wanting a man and marriage no matter what. Marriage and a husband is what He wants for you, but not when you're obsessing over it.

Trust what the Word says, and remain there, in His truth, and with that you will receive what He has promised you! Believe, He is always with us, even if we do not feel Him; He is there right beside you! Acknowledge His presence, and your life will change.

I pray that your heart will be changed, your mind renewed, and that you will live the fullness of the way He has called you to live—as a bride of the Lord—with Him as your Husband!

God bless you on this beautiful journey! Your life will never ever be the same!!

Chapter 12

Tina

"...The Lord says to you: Do not fear or be dismayed
at the sight of this vast multitude,
for the battle is not yours but God's."
—2 Chronicles 20:15

"He had to Give Me the God Makeover"

Tina, how did your restoration actually begin?

As far as I knew, we were "fine," but all too soon I realized that it was just in my head—my husband was not fine with anything. We had a lot of discussions, but he was always a quiet person and never said much; I was the one doing most, if not all, of the talking.

At one point, I became unemployed and bored; I turned a lot more of my attention on him. I commented at what time he arrived home and what time he left each morning. I became a person obsessed—argumentative, whining and complaining whenever he was around. This only kept him away more and more, trying to avoid me. When he was at home, he spent more and more time on his cell phone and made up reasons to stay at work or pick up more shifts to avoid me. Because he was never at home (and when he was we fought), I should have realized the end was about to happen.

Then one weekend, he just did not come home, and I went crazy. When he finally came home two days later, I got in his face demanding he answer me, but instead of the quiet person who just took what I dished out, he replied telling me to just "shut up," threw clothes into a suitcase and walked out of the house, never saying another word.

The next day, he sent me a very extensive message on my cell phone, telling me that he was leaving me for good, that he did not love me anymore and that he was not sure what he was going to do, but whatever he did, he wanted nothing to do with me, ever!

How did God change your situation, Tina, as you sought Him wholeheartedly?

This first week he was gone, I did not sleep, not at all. Instead, I stood at the window crying and waiting for him to open the front gate to our garden. This, of course, did not happen.

I guess I'd already suspected that there was OW, mainly because he'd recently changed the way he dressed. He often came home looking disheveled, and I could smell the perfume on his clothing. I would have accused him, but I didn't want to believe it, because I was so scared of losing him to someone else.

So on Monday morning, God spoke to my heart while in prayer. So, sleepily, I got up and searched the internet for something about marriage testimonies and found RMI. I read the RYM book in three days, prayed and fasted. I asked the Lord three times to show me and confirm His Purpose for our relationship, and He was faithful to show me His desire to restore our marriage, but first, He had to give me the "God Makeover."

As I began the course, my EH would come and go from our home—primarily to get more of his things. During those times that he went, I was much calmer and sweeter and never once asked him for anything, even though it hurt me inside to see him always leaving and walking out on me. But I'd learned to have a gentle and quiet spirit, and fasting helped to kill the flesh that would have been in his face demanding answers.

I also prayed to the Lord to keep me from knowing anything more about the OW, who she was, where she/they were and what they were doing. He was so faithful to do this for me!

As I was still unemployed, away from family and friends, away from the church, I began to realize that everything was the Lord's purpose, and I became content. "You have taken away my friends and my companions from me; darkness is my only company" (Psalm 88:18).

What principles, from God's Word (or through our resources), Tina, did the Lord teach you during this trial?

I learned to keep silent, speaking only to my HH in my heart about anything and everything.

Do not ask for help from your EH or anyone else; again, ask your HH, and He will cause it to happen.

Do not pursue him or even seek to know what he does and who the OW is, or anything about what is going on—keep your eyes on Him alone.

Pray for the hedge of thorns and for all truth to surface, for the adulterous woman to become bitter.

I discovered fasting and prayer for EH and OW's lives, for both of them to have an encounter with God.

Always answer that everything is fine, when anyone asked about us.

Daily reading of the Word is essential. (I became very hungry for the Word and for speaking to my HH.) Every time any sort of pain came, I would run to the Bible, talk to Him, and peace would come right back.

What were the most difficult times that God helped you through, Tina?

As I traveled my restoration journey, obeying the principle of "letting go" may have been the hardest. But also difficult was changing from panicking about being unemployed and instead embracing my situation, because it was part of His plan. I was already firm in the Lord's Promises, but before, I would never do what I knew was right, so I had to break that spirit of rebellion I'd had all my life and do what was right—like leave my EH alone. I also learned not to focus on the OW, because this wasn't about her but about me and Him.

I was becoming a different person, and everyone commented, which is about the same time my EH started to miss me and sent messages asking me to come back. When I got there, he was back from work and waiting in our house for me. I was afraid; everything was not ready; I knew I was not, but I thanked the Lord that He was with me when I went back home.

Tina, what was the "turning point" of your restoration?

The turning point, I may not be able to really explain. It was shortly after I was home and we'd had a few weeks of peace, when I discovered that he was talking to another woman, a person close to my family. Because I thought we were "restored," the news knocked me over.

Instead of being restored, it was actually part of my test, and I failed. I forgot all the principles I'd already learned and exposed myself as the

Pharisee I'd always been, as I exposed my husband's cheating to everyone! I slandered more people, before I was done, but then God in His infinite mercy reminded me of the book *How God Can and Will Restore Your Marriage*. I picked it up again and started doing my journal all over again, restarted the courses and stopped chasing my EH or restoration. That's when I realized I'd missed the part where I needed to fall for Him as my Husband, which is why I fell into the trap and failed my test.

God was faithful to test me again, once I'd wanted only the Lord, when "You're all I want; You're all I need; You're all I live for" was how I really felt. Asking me home again, I discovered that he had sought the same person, the same OW as he'd first been involved with, but this time I acted differently. I cared more about keeping my HH close and just delivered my EH into the hands of the Lord. I had no desire to keep the man who cheated, for as long as I do, I will never see the transformation in me or in our marriage that we need. My HH is more than enough, and once I realized and lived this way—everything turned around in my life.

Tell us HOW it happened, Tina. Did your husband just walk in the front door? Tina, did you suspect, or could you tell you were close to being restored?

I continued living in our home, keeping my HH first, and as much as anyone could ever claim, we are living happily ever after. I thank the Lord that He is with me, just as close as when I was on my restoration journey. I was wrong to have not sent my testimony, thinking it was not restored. But I am home, and even though He continues working in our lives, I realized He always will be. I came to my senses while reading a restored marriage testimony, when she'd confessed that it was a sin not giving God the praise He deserved, which motivated me to submit mine.

What rings true is that, even when there are trials after restoration, I believe that as long as our HH remains first, as Erin said in her videos, I know it's just the enemy trying to steal my peace and make me doubt what God has done.

Would you recommend any of our resources in particular that helped you, Tina?

I recommend EVERYONE read the *book How God Can and Will Restore Your Marriage*, which helped me in incredible ways! Knowing what to do in a crisis, before a marriage crisis hits, is so important. Why isn't it mandatory reading for every Christian and every church? Why is everyone so ignorant?

Today, I send Chapter 1 (click on the cover) to everyone that I know, whether they are needing help or not, and I have already received so many messages back thanking me. Glory to God! Soon I will be sending them Chapter 1 of *A Wise Woman workbook* and then sending them links to the Abundant Life courses.

Would you be interested in helping encourage other women, Tina?

Yes, of course, I already do that.

Either way, Tina, what kind of encouragement would you like to leave women with, in conclusion?

Do not continue to battle! This battle is God's; He will battle for us, while we get our "God Makeover." Even though it may seem difficult, try not to look at the circumstances, keep your focus on your Heavenly Husband, and everything else will fade away. I'm saying this, because that's what I need, too. I know we'll get all the love we need from only One source. Never take your eyes off the Lord, and soon you will be sharing your testimony with everyone too!!!

Chapter 13

Chen

"They looked to Him and were radiant,
and their faces will never be ashamed."
—Psalm 34:5

"OW's Husband sent me Intimate Photos of my Husband and his Wife!"

Chen, how did your restoration actually begin?

I knew our marriage was not going well. I was always a woman full of herself, selfish, hypocritical, a Pharisee, and I always wanted to be right about everything, never apologizing even if I was wrong. So we argued a lot, and when I became really angry I even hit him. Due to all of this, our relationship and his love for me, I could tell, was wearing off, and we began getting distant. At one point, when I first realized that he was distant, I tried to change things, but he was already a long way off emotionally from me.

It happened on a Monday, when he arrived home from work, he lay down next to me but said nothing, so I questioned him, and he tried to explain himself more—trying to tell me how he was feeling, the love he no longer felt. So I told him to just get out. I was so hurt and angry. So at the end of this same week, one day he just did not come home. I was shocked and collapsed on the floor, because I knew he'd decided to leave me for good.

How did God change your situation, Chen, as you sought Him wholeheartedly?

After a week of him not coming back, I began searching for testimonies of restored marriages online. I am convinced it was God who guided me to the RMI website, because the moment I read it was my Divine Appointment, I just knew He heard my cries.

I fell in love with everything I read. I bought and read the entire book *How God Can and Will Restore Your Marriage*, and I began to apply all the principles. I did not call him; I did not seek to know where he was, and as a result—God really supplied all my needs!

First, God gave me my Heavenly Husband, so I was not alone, and I found comfort and peace in my storm. My HH was with me in all moments of pain. Each and every night when my journey started, I cried a lot, prayed and repented while I journaled. I began praising God for each crisis, and I taught my children to do the same when they were hurt (whether from their father or from something at school). They began calling God their Heavenly Father and were no longer insecure or sad.

I found my Love Song early on and would wake up singing. I was always joyful, always happy. The old me was gone, and everyone told me I was glowing. Psalm 34:5, "They looked to Him and were radiant, and their faces will never be ashamed."

Not only were my children and I close, but God used this crisis for me to get close to my mother-in-law. We were never very close before, but God used this situation, not only mend our past (which was something my husband always asked me to do, but I was too proud, expecting her to apologize). I shared the lessons on having a Heavenly Husband with her (she was recently widowed), and she told me she was able to be happy again and move on with her life.

What principles, from God's Word (or through our resources), Chen, did the Lord teach you during this trial?

Immediately, when I began to read the first chapter of *How God Can and Will Restore Your Marriage,* the scales of my eyes fell, and I could see how wrong I was. What I knew I needed most was that I needed to put God first in my life. I was away from the presence of God in my life. Every Sunday night, I felt a huge emptiness inside me, and on several occasions I asked God to make a way for me to go back to His house, because before I was super active in the church, and I'd helped in several departments.

As I waited, He answered, when I saw we are His church! The moment I read about Restoration Fellowship, I applied, and my eyes were opened to how I'd robbed my husband of being my spiritual leader and the leader of our family.

The principles here are straight from the Word of God; they are not anyone's opinions. Each of the resources from the RMI website has taught me so much: being gentle and quiet, letting go, seeking God first, having a Heavenly Husband for ourselves, and helping our children understand and embrace their Heavenly Father (who goes everywhere with them, to protect and guide them).

It seems like every day more things are being added to us, like the benefit of reading Psalms and Proverbs every day, fasting (not just of food but other things like Facebook), not trying to do it on our own, asking our HH to do it, and when we need wisdom asking God. The first time I tried asking, I asked God to teach me how to feel the love of being my HH, because it just wasn't working for me. I was not getting it. Then I found the Love Song teaching and read the testimonies, and I just sensed it was about to happen to me!

I also asked God how to give a gentle answer to people who oppose what I was doing. I had a great aunt who strongly encouraged me to give up on my marriage, to move on. She is very involved in her church, and she was saying there's nothing wrong with divorce and remarriage. But just as Erin teaches, we need to be respectful, be agreeable, so I promised I would move on. So when she saw me all glowing, she was so happy that I'd found Someone! I moved on and found my HH.

There's just so much encouragement in Erin's books and offered free on these websites, which is why I became a partner. I made a prayer closet (on the side of the closet), where I could be alone (from the children— because they found me everywhere else), and it is my special place to meet with Him.

What were the most difficult times that God helped you through, Chen?

The hardest time I can remember is back when I'd hear my children calling for their dad, and he would never pick up or return their calls. Yet, this is what led to me asking God for wisdom and discovering the beauty of my children having their Heavenly Father.

There was also an extremely difficult moment, early on, when I woke up on a Sunday morning, and I received a message on Facebook from a stranger. When I opened it, there were intimate photos of my husband with an OW. I got very ill; I actually threw up, but I clung to God at that moment. Of course, I immediately let go and fasted Facebook after that, repenting that I hadn't done it sooner when it was taught in my lessons.

It was difficult, also, to know that my whole family had already seen the photos, and I was the last to know, because I had let go of the group of women I'd been hanging around with (We all gossipped horribly, so I knew I couldn't be part of that, nor could I judge them.) It was a family member who informed me of the OW's identity, that he got involved with a work colleague, which I was upset to know at first, but it was God who was preparing me.

The OW's husband called me, and that's when I found out it was he who sent the intimate photos of my husband and his wife to me and my family. With the teachings of RMI, I was able to not only explain that I preferred not to continue the conversation (once I found out who it was and what he wanted), but I also offered to send him a link to HopeAtLast.com, explaining that if he was hurting, he could find hope. (I don't know if he ever clicked on the link or read anything, but I just sensed it was what God wanted me to do.)

Chen, what was the "turning point" of your restoration?

God heard every one of my prayers, and I changed my prayers to simply praying His Word back to Him, "not returning void." This helped me let go completely, and then I began to find myself asking my HH to keep things just as they are. I not only didn't long for restoration, but I also began to not want it at all. That's when I read what Erin said, that it's not about what we want, but us wanting His perfect plan. This was a pivotal moment in my journey.

Just as so many women say in their restored marriage testimonies, it was less than a week after I no longer wanted restoration when I got several messages on my cell phone from my EH, saying that he wanted to talk to me, if I would please answer him. I waited, because I didn't know what to say and wasn't sure I was ready. So then he called and asked me if we could meet to talk, so I said okay. He told me he'd meet me at my work (which is "so God," because my coworkers told me it would never happen, that he'd never come back).

That evening, he took me to the best restaurant by the lake. We mostly talked about the children and his work, and then he finally told me that he did not know what I wanted for my life, that he could see I was very happy. Then he said, "Chen, I just want my family back; I want you back in my life," and he kissed me, and we both began to cry.

Tell us HOW it happened, Chen. Did your husband just walk in the front door? Chen, did you suspect, or could you tell you were close to being restored?

I was not discouraged, when he did not come home immediately that night, but whenever he came over, he was always nice and always pleasant. What's amazing is that I didn't care and was basically relieved he wasn't moving back in. He always left saying that he would come back soon and that he did not know what I was doing but encouraged me to continue whatever I was doing, because it was working. I wasn't sure if he was talking about my prayers or how I'd changed.

It happened this past Father's Day, when he came back with all of his things. I did not suspect anything that day; he just called and asked where we were. I said, "At home," and just a half an hour later, he came walking in and said to me and the children, "I'm back home. I'm home for good."

Would you recommend any of our resources in particular that helped you, Chen?

I highly recommend the *book How God Can and Will Restore Your Marriage*. I also recommend the courses that I am still doing every morning, so that I can continue to change more and more and continue to be the bride of my Beloved Heavenly Husband. I also continue to study *A Wise Woman* that He'd led me to begin just weeks before my restoration.

Would you be interested in helping encourage other women, Chen?

Yes, I am very interested in helping other women.

Either way, Chen, what kind of encouragement would you like to leave women with, in conclusion?

Dear brides, trust in God and follow all the principles written in all the books, and take the courses to journal this amazing journey you're on. Everything here is directly from the Bible; everything is the pure Word of God for us.

Love God with all your heart, because His plan is what's best for you. God loves us and sent His Son, not just to be our Savior when we die, like Erin says, but in order for us to live life abundantly.

Our HH wants to see us happy; this is what allows God to finish what He started and also draws others to want to know Him. If you are a quarrelsome woman right now, like I was, it will only lead you to destroy your own house. With His love, you can become a loving, Godly woman, because it's only through His love that you can change.

"...No eye has seen, nor ear heard, nor the heart of man imagined, what God has prepared for those who love Him" (1 Corinthians 2:9 ESV).

Chapter 14

Esmée

"He who trusts in his own heart is a fool,
But he who walks wisely will be delivered."
—Proverbs 28:26

"Crushed, but Trusting in Him, Alone"

Translated from French

Esmée, how did your restoration actually begin?

After he left me, I was crushed. A friend took me in, took charge and hosted me for two weeks.

Then we went to pray every day, then several times a week. After that, I prayed alone.

How did God change your situation, Esmée, as you sought Him wholeheartedly?

First, God, in my prayers, gave me faith. I struggled with Envy. Then, I met people who prayed for me, for us as a couple, and for our family and children. I went to rescue prayers. I prayed for my deliverance, but also his.

One day, on my knees, I felt in my heart God talk to me: it was very clear: "Are you really going to follow Me now?"

What principles, from God's Word (or through our resources), Esmée, did the Lord teach you during this trial?

He asked me through His Word to choose Him, not to be unfaithful to Him anymore. I saw words like "I saw his conduct, but I will heal him."

One day I asked, "Lord, I see how great my sin is, the harm that I did to him, harm that I did to myself by refusing to be submissive. Give us a chance, not at all because of my merits; I have none, and I see how much I've done wrong! But because of your sacrifice—the sacrifice of You on the cross."

It was not a theoretical understanding ...nor because of what I remembered that I had been told (I thought I was being stupid.) I thought I was going to ask Him without any merit—on the merit of Him, on the fact that He had already paid. [I felt this might be wrong/ too bold.] YET...there, in my heart, clearly, I heard Him saying "On the contrary, you finally really understand."

Handwritten margin note: "Not because of who I am, but because of what You've done, not because of what I've done, but because of who You are."

What were the most difficult times that God helped you through, Esmée?

The desire to die.

The day my earthly husband said "I love you, I'm coming back," but on the way, he cheated on me....

And I felt it.

I prayed for him to tell me the truth about what he did. It was a moment of pure grace; I could forgive—to see him, who he is, with compassion. We stayed talking to me for four hours on the phone. But he hung up. Then, at the appointed meeting place, he rejected me, and he told me it was finally over between us. I tried to convince him...but for him, it was final, over.

When I got home, I screamed. I got scared. My EH even heard me scream, because he was at the park a few houses away. I was inconsolable in my distress. I saw everything I had was gone. The loss was deep.

I went to the psychiatric hospital. There I was helped by a woman who prayed with me, who was a real guardian angel!!!! She stayed until the doctor arrived. He told me that I was normal, I didn't need to be hospitalized.

At peace again, to my earthly husband, I sent a text saying that I respected his decision. But I did not stay calm afterwards. It was a very, very hard time. Then I remained quiet.

Esmée, what was the "turning point" of your restoration?

Two weeks after his total rejection and my total silence, remaining quiet (using it as a fast), he phoned to find out how I was (I did not expect it at all!). I went to church and when I came back, he wanted to see me, and he wanted to hold my hand. I refused, kindly. I told him, "I have a life in front of me. I put my Heavenly Husband in first place now..." And we really talked for the first time ...

He said to me "I had suffered too much in our marriage, I did not have the strength to leave, so I wanted to give you courage to leave me; so that you could go away, by me deceiving you." "But," said he, "it was the first time in my life that I met someone who knew how to forgive, like you just forgave me."

Afterwards, he courted me for weeks. We confessed our love just by holding hands... without commitment. He told me, "If we had kept this child...(I was not Christian, I did this stupidity; I was then in deep depression, at the very beginning of our relationship. I took medication; there was risk of disability) . . . He said, "if we had kept it, I would have married you."

I took courses of Bible study, as a concrete act of my commitment to God (what He hoped for, waited for), and this study gave me a great peace. I was ready to wait for years for my husband (hoping it was him). This detachment brought us closer. I wanted to base things on the heart!

He still hesitated sometimes, and once he said to me, "How can you be jealous? You have no rights over me" and I answered, "I may have no right to you, or to be jealous; it's true! You are right. Because the foundation is trust. But if you refuse faithfulness, then I prefer to stop everything and cut off all contact." God comes first. I wanted to build on GOD's values. So I said, "Love is a decision, decide for yourself." He told me he wanted to be faithful.

Tell us HOW it happened, Esmée. Did your man just walk in the front door? Esmée, did you suspect or could you tell you were close to being restored?

Being restored was a struggle, to accept and trust only my God, and I still do, but I saw him change!!!!!!!! soften!!!!!!! Despite struggles, I saw Him take care of him. Today I really see God at work in both our lives!

I pray that my own heart is softened by His presence! I need to pray often and let myself be loved by Him, in order to achieve what He has for me, for us.

Would you recommend any of our resources in particular that helped you, Esmée?

-Marital help from *How God Can and Will Restore Your Marriage* also *A Wise Woman*. All of the *By the Word of Their Testimonies*, and going through online courses. Daily Encourager

-Teachings

-Bible

-prayers of deliverance

-thankfulness

-to be independent of anyone but my Heavenly Husband

-the sweetness, the calm, the listening, of my Heavenly Husband

Would you be interested in helping encourage other women, Esmée?

Yes

Whoever trusts his own thoughts is just a fool, but whoever directs his course according to wisdom will escape the dangers (Proverbs 28:26).

As much as the sky is high above the earth, so are my ways elevated above your ways, and so are my thoughts high above yours (Isaiah 55:9)

Philippians 4... Do not worry about anything; but in all things make known your needs to God through prayers and supplications, with actions thanksgiving. And the peace of God, which surpasses all understanding, will keep your hearts and your thoughts in Jesus Christ.

Either way, Esmée, what kind of encouragement would you like to leave women with, in conclusion?

To forgive sins, wanderings, errors and regrets, put them at the foot of the cross.

Pray for Him to work in your heart. Forgive all, (make a list) including yourself, and make the decision to follow Him!

It is the heart of stone that separates or divides. Let your Heavenly Husband make of your heart a heart of flesh.

Even though it can hurt sometimes, He can give you His peace and His consolation, as no man could do it better!

Do not put your man first. He may be lost.

Bless Him. Praise God.

Do in your life what is right in the eyes of God: put yourself in right standing with God.

The most difficult thing I had to do: Give on your way beyond your pain. What we most desire deep in our heart is communion. Even though it did not cost me, what I thought was a weakness healed me, and was not a defeat, but each time a Victory.

Even though it cost me, what I thought was a weakness "to go to His arms", still angry, when He invited me there to be embraced) He healed me, and was not a defeat, but each time a Victory—that of sacrificing my ego for the love (of the heart) that my Heavenly Husband proposed to me.

Anger = hurt or fear (for me)
 Bring it to Him!
I remember Him asking me, when I felt stuck in a spiral,
 "Why are you angry?"
I couldn't close the distance with Him until I gave Him
those hot, angry tears and let Him hold me.
 (Journal entries from 8/13/23 - 8/15/23)

Chapter 15

Claire

"Your adornment must not be merely external…
but let it be the hidden person of the heart,
with the imperishable quality of a
gentle and quiet spirit,
which is precious in the sight of God."
—1 Peter 3:3-4

"After We were Restored the Enemy Attacked Even More"

Claire, how did your restoration actually begin?

I thought my marriage was solid and strong, until my husband began commuting and working in another city, which was about two hours away. That's where he got involved with the OW and my world fell apart. After only commuting for a few months, he arrived home one weekend and said he wanted to separate. I was shocked. We had been having issues for almost four years. We were together for twelve years (being married only six years), after living together. Now, I know that I'd built my marriage on sinking sand, on sin, and because of this, my world ended when all this happened.

After he packed and left home, I found out that the OW had come to town with him, and they left together. When he left me, left us, he was like someone I didn't even know. He didn't even care about anything but his happiness and being with this woman. He didn't care to know how we would pay the bills or rent. He didn't even talk to our daughter, who asked about him every day. She was always very attached to him, a real daddy's girl. The highlight of her day was when he came home from work.

How did God change your situation, Claire, as you sought Him wholeheartedly?

As soon as he left, God had already placed a person I had not even expected into my life an ex-wife of one of my husband's co-workers. I already knew her, but we had no relationship; certainly, we weren't friends. Yet one day, she approached me, when she saw me in the grocery store, and told me about how she'd found peace when her husband cheated on her that she was living the Abundant Life. I didn't really want to just move on; I honestly didn't know what I wanted. So I agreed to go have coffee with her, and she told me about this FREE course she was taking online. I could see she was glowing, and I was intrigued, but I was also a bit afraid of what she'd gotten into.

I was so very hurt, so sad, that I just cried nonstop. I lost close to thirty pounds in the first month I just couldn't eat. I didn't go out; I just cried. This ex-wife I mentioned contacted me again and shared a link to purchase restored marriage *Testimonies*, from several eBooks. I'd been searching the internet for testimonials of restored marriages, and I found RMI again. So I thought, "this must be God," so I downloaded the book *How God Can and Will Restore Your Marriage*. I started reading it, and it was then that God broke me. I saw how wrong I was as a wife and mother. Prior to this, I thought it was all my husband's fault and blamed everything on him and the OW.

"perspectacles"

It clicked right away. I changed my thinking and my way of seeing things. From there, I learned to pray the right way. I prayed with my heart full of thanksgiving, and I no longer pleaded with God to change my husband. I wanted to be changed, and that's when I read something in the Encourager that led me to begin taking the Finding the Abundant Life course, and I knew, I just knew, what my new friend was trying to tell me!

After the third FAL chapter, my husband called, and we began talking by phone. He'd sneak away from the OW to find out how I was. In the beginning, when he first tried calling, it almost always ended in huge arguments and nasty fights. But once I had a gentle and quiet spirit, I no longer was desperate. I know now (because he told me after we restored) that when he thought he was losing me, he got scared, which he said is why he called me all the time.

"As long as it takes" is what I told God, when I thought of restoration. Having a close friend who was also His bride helped me be able to embrace my new life and let go. I learned much in such a short amount of time! When my EH wanted to sell our house, I agreed quickly and happily moved in with my father. We ultimately stayed there for only two months, but I didn't care if it took years. I was living my abundant life as His bride, and I was just happy.

As God would have it, my EH only lived with the OW about a month, and then she kicked him out, after she caught him calling me. The more I became closer to my Beloved and let God restore my marriage (if that was His will for my life), the more my husband called, came by and asked about things in my life. I was able to tell him how happy I was in my new life as a bride.

What principles, from God's Word (or through our resources), Claire, did the Lord teach you during this trial?

I learned that first, we have to focus on ourselves and that we can't change ourselves, either. Only God can change us, through the washing of His Word and the love we get from our HH. When we accept this as truth and let ourselves be broken, then He can start to heal us through His Word and His love. God's ways are perfect. He takes care of every detail. The RYM book is great. I purchased a case and have given it out to many friends.

Before my best friend's marriage collapsed, I wanted to help her, so I gave her one of the books. Yet, she didn't really think she needed restoring. So we began doing A Wise Woman, course 3, together, and she was able to see how little she knew about being a wife and mother. The online lessons, along with the testimonies. helped me and helped her too.

Everything you offer helps us emotionally as women. Marriage problems are very painful, when we lose someone who we love and who we thought loved us too. I never lost anyone in my life before this. But I believe the pain is necessary to get our attention. I wanted to die, so I wouldn't have to go through it. Soon, I changed my mind, when I remembered I had a little girl who needed me. All I can say is how thankful I am that someone reached out to me, offering me hope. As I said, I knew about RMI, but I really didn't know what it was all about. This is why I try to reach out and let women know what I've come through, and I offer my support to get them set on the right path and journey.

We have to be the kind of wives God sees as precious, Wise Women. I didn't know that was anything God was interested in. I had no understanding of the Word, even though I'd grown up in the church. What I learned here, in just a couple of weeks, was enough for me to change my life forever. My prayers were heard. God answered me quickly, when I cried out to Him. Many times a day, I mention something to my Beloved, and sometimes a response happens the very next day! He is wonderful!!!

What were the most difficult times that God helped you through, Claire?

There were many. The beginning was the hardest. You discover so many of your faults early on in your journey. There are many things that you, yourself, contributed to destroy your own life; it is devastating. The worst is when the enemy attacks you, using your husband, through words of hate, void of love. Contempt is expressed; the hate wall is erected. It's terrible that it appears like he's so good and happy, while we're so destroyed

Claire, what was the "turning point" of your restoration?

More than three times, I thought about giving up. I asked God to take away the feeling I had for my husband. I didn't want to suffer anymore. But the Lord gave me dreams of when we were together and happy, and I woke up with new hope. Then, I realized God wanted me to give up and give it to Him. As a Bride, the pain melts away.

A week after I became my HH's bride, my husband started calling me. When he called, I was always calm, always full of joy. I didn't respond curtly or sarcastically, which always had created more friction between us. I believe most women do this, too. Occasionally, he would be rude, but even then, I never got upset. It wasn't because I was hiding it either. I just no longer reacted, because I had a Lover.

I knew I was close to restoration. In a matter of three days, he called me about ten times a day. He told me he purchased a new car and had a new job. Then one week, everything changed. He rented a lovely home by the beach and called us, asking us if we wanted to come live with him. It was all so sudden! The transition was not easy. It was difficult to have as much time with my HH as I'd come to enjoy. Also, after we were restored, the enemy attacked me/us even more. I just held tight to my HH, when my EH tried to go back to the OW. But she didn't want him, which was such a shock. I knew it was God turning her heart away from my EH.

As you say to us, over and over again, it's after our husbands are back that it gets difficult. The enemy is just waiting around for a crack. Yet, if we remain steadfast to our First Love, then there is nothing anyone can do to harm us.

Tell us HOW it happened, Claire. Did your husband just walk in the front door? Claire, did you suspect or could you tell you were close to being restored?

He called me and said everything was all wrong. Each time we talked, it was clear he wanted to be a family again. He asked for forgiveness almost every time we talked, which I know is not at all common. I believe this is because I told God I didn't care if he ever asked for forgiveness.

As I already said, after my husband got a new job, he asked us to move in with him. I thank God we are more than fine now. Another three times, so far, the enemy has already tried to break us up. Yet, each time I find myself closer to my HH, and that, in turn, causes my husband to get closer to me, and our relationship as a married couple becomes stronger.

Would you recommend any of our resources in particular that helped you, Claire?

All of them!! The books and online courses, the videos, and all you offer for FREE is wonderful. Read Psalms & Proverbs. Follow and listen to God, only. The people around you do not know what is deep in your heart. God only knows what's best for us, He will lead us to an abundant life.

Would you be interested in helping encourage other women, Claire?

Yes, it's important that we reach out and be willing to make ourselves available to women who are facing marriage crisis. I have Become a Minister, ministering more in my neighborhood than online so far.

Either way, Claire, what kind of encouragement would you like to leave women with, in conclusion?

Once the contentious woman is gone, the only way she won't come back is to become His bride. The enemy uses our own husbands to hurt us with words, unfaithfulness and an uncaring attitude. As Erin says, don't snoop around. The only way to be at peace is to let go and let God restore your life and marriage. Your husband is only won without a word. Let Him take care of every detail. Focus on your relationship with your HH.

Chapter 16

Delilah

"Love is patient, love is kind and is not jealous;
love does not brag and is not arrogant...
bears all things, believes all things,
hopes all things, endures all things."
—1 Corinthians 13:4-7

"RMI's "Absurd" Principles Became My Lifeline"

Delilah, how did your restoration actually begin?

My husband and I were very happy during our fifteen-year relationship, from when we first started dating and got engaged to when we first got married. But then, shortly after we married, I found out that he'd gotten involved with a "friend" from work. At first, I just cried and wanted so much to forgive him and help him out of this situation.

When I confronted him, he was so very sorry, and he cried a lot, but because he continued working at the same company, along with the OW, I just knew it would continue. It did. Soon after, my EH moved out, and during our first separation, they did not move in together as a couple. They were dating. I already knew about RMI, because a friend had introduced me, but I found it absurd to follow some of the principles in the book *How God Can and Will Restore Your Marriage*. I was alone in prayer (with a forgiving heart), and it was a month after the separation that God used to get my attention, when my husband returned to our home.

After two months, he was still working with the OW, and he left home again for our second separation. This was when I started acting like every jealous wife, by making anonymous calls, locking him out of a lot of online stuff, and a lot more "silly woman" nonsense—ultimately tearing my house down completely. This time, I completely threw my husband into the OW's arms, and they decided to move in and live together.

After three months of living apart, my husband decided to return to our house; he said he missed his son and his wife very much and felt God calling him to return to his family and His presence. This time, everything seemed to be going very well for us. We decided to move back to our small town, where we'd met. He quit his job where the OW worked, got a job in our hometown, and we were living happily — or so I thought. Then, out of nowhere, he threatened to commit suicide. From that moment on, he only thought about her, and I started to realize that I was always the reason for our separation. When he told me that he couldn't stop thinking about the OW and that he would be going back to her, I realized that I would never be able to trust him again.

It was at this moment, when our third separation took place, that everything went wrong. My husband went back to the OW, while my son and I continued living in the same small town. My world collapsed; this time, because we had moved away from everyone, my son was enrolled in a new school, and I was alone, no longer in control. Finally, God got my attention, and all of RMI's "absurd" principles became my lifeline.

How did God change your situation, Delilah, as you sought Him wholeheartedly?

At that moment, I began to realize that I was doing everything wrong; I had no idea what God had for me. I regretted never sending a restored marriage testimony, but since I'd done it in my own strength, using the world's tactics, it would never have been honoring God.

It was then that I started to put into practice every single thing I had been reading in the book, and I also began not just skimming over the courses — I began journalling and pouring my heart out to God. I was able to confess and really speak to Him about how I was feeling, and I focused on the principles in each lesson. Immediately, I could see God was working in my life in a very special way. Mainly, I started to see my husband with other eyes of love, patience, kindness, etc. from 1 Corinthians 13. This happened almost immediately, when I started the first Fellowship Course, and I met my HH during Finding the Abundant Life. I stopped listening to "Those Voices" and heard Him say "You're Beautiful!!" Very soon, I was "Utterly Lovesick"!!

What principles, from God's Word (or through our resources), Delilah, did the Lord teach you during this trial?

God helped me understand that I could live very well without my earthly husband, so I became less controlling and manipulating to everyone in my life, no longer striving to get what I "thought" I needed. I had all I needed or wanted in Him. I began to put my HH first in my life; everything I do is about Him. I live for Him. It was such a shock that the absence of my earthly husband began to become completely insignificant, while all bitterness and anguish over the memories and disappointments began to dissolve away. God began to heal me of everything, as I asked Him and allowed Him to do that in every area of my life. I no longer felt the pain of separation or betrayal and all that I was made to suffer. That foolish woman who talked too much, thankfully, died. I did not judge my husband, did not seek him, nor seek money from him, and I allowed myself to be intimate with him when he came to visit, even knowing that he was already living with another woman, since we were still legally married.

What were the most difficult times that God helped you through, Delilah?

The most difficult time was probably when the OW posted several pictures of them on several social networks, and friends of my son began to make fun of him. It was also difficult when my son saw them walking along the street holding hands, and then my husband used this situation to blame it on me. It hurt, when he told our son that I was missing important aspects of what a wife should be, so he had to be with someone else.

Thankfully, I'd learned from RMI to take full responsibility (rather than argue or defend myself) and lay it as my Lover's feet. I felt at peace, and soon after, both my husband and son began to praise me, just as it says will happen in Proverbs 31.

Delilah, what was the "turning point" of your restoration?

This time, I figured it would take a long time for him to come back home, mainly because I was more than "fine without him." But I was wrong again. My husband took our son out alone, just him and our son, and the following day he sent me a text message saying that he missed me very much. Soon after, he asked me out on a date that led to us being intimate. While he was leaving, he took hold of my hands and tearfully begged me to pray for him, because he was miserable and wanted out of the way he was living. He said he could no longer stand to be away from his family and loathed the OW.

Tell us HOW it happened, Delilah. Did your husband just walk in the front door? Delilah, did you suspect or could you tell you were close to being restored?

Yes, it happened without warning. On a sunny Saturday, my son and I were getting ready to go out to breakfast, when he appeared. On the porch were bags full of all his clothes, and shoes, and personal belongings. After almost four months of being separated the third time—GOD restored our marriage. I knew I didn't need to try to keep him home, or monitor him, or control anything. I just needed to keep my HH first and go to Him with all my needs or concerns.

After he was home for five months, he told me how different I was and how life for him was so much easier, because I'd changed. He wanted to know how I'd done it, so I told him about RMI, and I told him they'd sent a gift for him to make changes—but only if he was interested. So far, every night he's stayed up reading *A Wise Man* in bed. Talk about a miracle I thought I'd never see!!

Would you recommend any of our resources in particular that helped you, Delilah?

How God Can and Will Restore Your Marriage also begin to study *A Wise Woman*. Do the FREE online courses; pour your heart into the journals, and, if you want the pain to stop, take the Abundant Life courses.

Would you be interested in helping encourage other women, Delilah?

Yes

Either way, Delilah, what kind of encouragement would you like to leave women with, in conclusion?

Don't try to do this yourself. Don't ever think anything in any of the courses is absurd (like I did), so you will be spared a lot of time of suffering, and you will begin to live life abundantly. No matter what your situation is, God is faithful to remake you and give you the miracle of a restored marriage and an abundant life. God is the God of miracles!!

Delight in the Lord; trust in Him and the more He will do for you!!!!!

Chapter 17

Lale

"He who conceals his transgressions
will not prosper,
But he who confesses and forsakes them
will find compassion."
—Proverbs 28:26

"I Had to Confess My Infidelity"

I want to thank my God for all that He has done for me. Six months ago, my husband started a new job in another country. I was supposed to join him after two months, but as soon as he got there, he started to act differently, and I became afraid and jealous. We had several arguments, and one month after he left, he said he wasn't coming back and he didn't want me there with him. He said our marriage had many problems and he didn't even know why he married me, because he wasn't sure if he had loved me from the very beginning.

Of course, I was heartbroken. I became really depressed, and I didn't know what to do. I already had quit my job to be with him, and now I was lonely and without any money to support myself. My husband said that he didn't have money to send me, and that was it. I was left with all the bills (rent, phones, credit cards, etc.). He said he was looking for somebody else to love and wanted to be loved, and I wasn't welcome where he was, because at any time another person could be in the picture.

I miraculously I found RMI, out of nowhere. I wasn't even looking for the site on my phone. I don't remember exactly what I typed, but there it was! As soon as I saw it, I started to take the online courses, one after the other. It opened my eyes, and I was able to see my mistakes and failures.

I changed all the wrongs immediately. I didn't beg as before, nor call or ask for money as before.

I used all my energy to focus on the books I'd ordered from *Encouraging Bookstore*, and on your free courses, and I began to Read through the Bible. I started to pray fervently, asking God to provide for my needs. I learned and began Tithing to my storehouse from money I earned cleaning a few houses in my building. I asked my Heavenly Husband, if it was His will, to have my husband begin paying the bills.

My earthly husband started to focus his attention on me after some months. He called me often and asked me about the bills, and I just answered his questions honestly, but I never asked him for anything. Then one day, he said, "I'll send you some money each week," and he did.

Then, in one of the courses, Erin said if we ever had been unfaithful, we had to confess this to our spouse (Proverbs 28:13). I thought, "No way!" It happened 4 years ago, and nobody knew about it, except for me and the other guy. My husband will never forget that. So I just turned the page, and forgot about it. Some weeks later, I read in the online courses that no matter how long ago the infidelity happened, I had to confess. So I started to panic. I prayed, to ask God to show me His will (not Erin's). Then, one day at church, a person asked me to participate on the platform by reading a verse. Then I saw the verse was: "He who conceals his transgressions will not prosper, but he who confesses and forsakes them will find compassion"!!!

Reading Proverbs 28:13, I immediately thought of my infidelity, and I said, "Ok God, You need to confirm this once again, like Gideon's story." The next day I said, "I'm going to read my Bible, and if it's true that You, God, want me to tell my EH today, let me know." So I opened the Psalms and Proverbs reading. I stopped when I saw Psalm 51 that said at the beginning, "A Psalm of David, when Nathan the prophet came to him, after he had gone in to Bathsheba." That was the answer for me. If David committed adultery and later was confronted by Nathan, I had to obey, or I would be confronted by God. So I confessed to my husband by phone. He was shocked and sooo hurt. He didn't say much, but days later, he asked for a divorce. I just prayed and stayed faithful to God's will. My EH stopped sending money, but my HH sent me a job.

I honestly didn't know what God did, but as always, He never fails.

My husband just returned home 2 weeks ago, and he decided not to leave again. I keep praising Him for not letting another woman get into our lives and for my EH who hugs me all night. My Jesus forgave me, and so did my EH, too.

I love You with all my heart and long to spend every moment with You, My Love!!

Here are a few Bible Verses He gave me during my journey.

"Therefore the LORD longs to be gracious to you, and therefore He WAITS on high to have compassion on you For the LORD is a God of justice; How blessed are all those who long for Him" (Isaiah 30:18).

"I remain confident of this: I will see the goodness of the Lord in the land of the living. Wait for the Lord; be strong and take heart and wait for the Lord" (Psalm 27:13-14).

"Now all glory to God, who is able, through his mighty power at work within us, to accomplish infinitely more than we can ask or think" (Ephesians 3:20).

"For no matter how many promises God has made, they are 'Yes' in Christ. And so, through him the 'Amen' is spoken by us to the glory of God. Now it is God who makes both us and you stand firm in Christ" (2 Corinthians 1:20-21).

"Be still, and know that I am God; I will be exalted among the nations, I will be exalted in the earth" (Psalm 46:10).

"Trust in the LORD with all your heart and do not lean on your own understanding. In all your ways acknowledge Him, and He will make your paths straight" (Proverbs 3:4-6).

Chapter 18

Quinn

"…In everything give thanks;
for this is God's will for you in Christ Jesus."
— 1 Thessalonians 5:18

"It Was Like Watching a Movie of My Life"

Quinn, how did your restoration actually begin?

One afternoon in August, three years ago, I was sitting on my couch with a victim mentality crying, "Why me God?!" Believing that nothing that was happening was my fault—when suddenly, it was like watching a movie of my life from the moment I turned my back on God. How ugly I'd become! I had become a quarrelsome, contentious woman, who never stopped talking and did not know how to listen. I was the foolish woman who was tearing down her own house! And in the midst of that storm came my Beloved Savior, and immediately my mind came to Proverbs 3. So I ran to my Bible and read that chapter, and verses 5, 6 and 7 pierced my soul!

"Trust in the Lord with all your heart And do not lean on your own understanding. In all your ways acknowledge Him, And He will make your paths straight. Do not be wise in your own eyes; Fear the Lord and turn away from evil" (Proverbs 3:5-7).

I fell on my knees...that day, I thought it was the bluest, greyest day of my life, and then, it changed to become the most colorful and important of all. My Beloved Savior came to my rescue!!

How did God change your situation, Quinn, as you sought Him wholeheartedly?

God invited me on this journey of restoration, which I accepted, and He began to teach wonderful and very important principles. Then came the moment when I felt so good with God; I thought and I said, "All is good, Lord; have Your will in my life. You personally invited me on this trip with You, and I know now that I never want to be away from You anymore. I dedicate myself to being alone with You and falling in love more and more. I am trusting You and Your promises." All along, He was working, even when I did not see or understand it, and soon I began to see changes taking place.

What principles, from God's Word (or through our resources), Quinn, did the Lord teach you during this trial?

1) To give Him the first place in everything.

2) To change things as He taught me from His Word. Read through the Bible

3) To trust His promises, not what I saw or felt. Proverbs 3:5

4) To look only at Him and not at the circumstances surrounding me.

5) To hear Him alone and not the voices that allowed the enemy to frighten me.

6) To give thanks for everything—because my whole life is led by Him, and He always has a purpose in every road that He takes me on. 1 Thessalonians 5:18

What were the most difficult times that God helped you through, Quinn?

It was most difficult when I had to leave my house, especially when the Christmas holidays came and I was away, full of sadness. But God always made me see that everything was directed by Him and His plans are always better. "Many plans are in a man's heart, But the counsel of the Lord will stand" (Proverbs 19:21). Besides having had a relationship that failed (something I thought would never happen), I'd gotten so close to Him and learned to rejoice in His presence every moment.

Quinn, what was the "turning point" of your restoration?

I was at my father's house, and, out of nowhere, a guy I had not seen in years appeared in my life. When we were young, he'd said he was in love with me. He had heard that I had separated and was living at my father's house. The next day, my sister told me, "He is now a widower and you are alone." I said, "No, I am not alone. I know that God rescued me and my life is in His hands and I hope to see His glory in this situation." Could this be His plan?

The next day, I met up with my sister, and she started talking about this guy's feelings towards me. Immediately I told her, "No; I do not want to hear this, and I forbid you from ever mentioning him to me again." I was emphatic, "I do not care; I'm not available; I am on a journey of restoration. God has directed and guided me. I have left my future in His hands. I know my status as separated is only temporary—because my life and my home will be restored."

That all happened on December 23, and just two days later, on Christmas day, my husband sent me a text saying, "I miss you, and I realized that I really love you"! I just praised God. When reading the text, I knew that without a doubt my faithfulness to Him had let Him take me on the next step in my journey, and everything I endured and my faithfulness was now being rewarded. If I had listened to the voice of the enemy, all would have been lost. But I decided to trust God and His promises!!

Tell us HOW it happened, Quinn. Did your husband just walk in the front door? Quinn, did you suspect or could you tell you were close to being restored?

After he sent the text, he invited me to lunch, and that was my chance to apologize and let him see God in me.

My father's house is remote, far from the city, and in this very cold climate, living at his home was making me sick. So by mid-January, one day, my husband came over and began to pack up my things. I asked, "What are you doing?" And he said, "Today you are coming home."

Could I see or suspected that I was close to being restored? No. I simply trusted God and His promises. Every day, I tell everyone I meet that those who trust in God are never ashamed. My confidence was, and is, placed in Him Who can do everything.

Would you recommend any of our resources in particular that helped you, Quinn?

My first recommendation is to be guided directly by God and accept this journey of restoration, and stay consistent to travel this journey with Him.

In particular, I'd recommend all your online courses that taught me a lot, and I know it was God speaking to me through each lesson. I'd make sure it was Him guiding me, because before I started each lesson, I would say, "Show me Your power, as I know this comes from You." Surely God put this material in my hands.

Do you have favorite Bible verses you would like to share with women who read your testimony? Or promises he gave you?

"Trust in the Lord with all your heart and lean not on your own understanding" (Proverbs 3:5).

"Behold, I will do a new thing, now it springs forth, do you not perceive? Again I will make way in the wilderness and rivers in the dry land" (Isaiah 43:19).

"I waited patiently for the Lord; and he inclined to me and heard my cry" (Psalms 40:1).

"But I have against you that you left your first love" (Rev. 2:4).

"Even there shall thy hand lead and thy right hand shall hold me" (Psalms 139:10).

Would you be interested in helping encourage other women, Quinn?

Yes

Either way, Quinn, what kind of encouragement would you like to leave women with, in conclusion?

First, your goal is to fall in love more and more with your Heavenly Husband. Each day, achieving a relationship with Him as you never imagined that you'd want or would be possible. Next, trust in Him and His promises; His Word does not return void (Isaiah 55:11). He knows our situations and will handle everything. Lastly, something very important, once you have decided to take this trip, this journey with Him, you must be firmly committed, without hesitation, and you must close your ears to the voices that the enemy will surely use against you. If you believe, you will see His glory.

Chapter 19

Agustina

"Older women likewise are to be reverent in their behavior...
encourage the young women to love their husbands,
to love their children, to be sensible, pure, workers at home,
kind, being subject to their own husbands,
so that the word of God will not be dishonored."
— 1 Titus 2:3-5

"I Stopped All My Stupid Speeches"

Agustina, how did your restoration actually begin?

Three years ago, my husband started to distance himself from me. We were married very young; we were both only 16-years-old, so we started out in a very difficult situation. We came from very different families. I am a pastor's daughter, and he is a deacon's son, but I was raised very strictly. I spent most of my time in church, while he stopped going to church after his parents stopped forcing him.

Early on when we met, I discovered that he enjoyed pornography (which he promised, when we married, wasn't something he was still addicted to). Later, I found out he'd never stopped.

After struggling to hold our marriage together, he just stopped caring about me and spent too much time on the computer—sometimes all night long until dawn. Our intimacy was nonexistent. I started praying, asking God to show me what was going on. One day, when my husband went to the store and left his social network open, I saw everything I didn't want to see!! At first, I believed God had shown me (but now I know it was the enemy tempting me). I read conversations with friends, some with women or about other women, that shook me. Continuing to play into the enemy's schemes (who is out to "kill, steal and destroy" us), I confronted my husband, and he denied it, but I knew; I just knew.

Instead of seeking God, I tried to discuss and talk about it with him, more and more. Rather than helping, he just began leaving home, so he didn't have me pressing him. Even on our wedding anniversary, he was gone, never even acknowledging the day. It was then that I felt I'd lost my husband for good. My life was a mess.

How did God change your situation, Agustina, as you sought Him wholeheartedly?

I started worrying about my future and searching the internet for something about restored marriages, and I found RMI. I knew the story of Erin, but I had no idea she had a book. By a miracle of the Lord, a woman from my church handed me the books *How God Can and Will Restore Your Marriage* and *A Wise Woman builds her house, by a fool who first built on sinking sand*. She told me it had saved her marriage and that she kept these books in the trunk of her car to give out! I still have no idea how she knew I'd asked God to show me how I could get my hands on a book!

It didn't take long for me to realize that I was completely wrong. I'd grown up in the church with parents as pastors, and yet I was ignorant about everything that God's Word said about marriage, about anything. How is that even possible, I wondered?

First, I was not truly seeking God for my answers, nor was He at the center of my life. All my life, I'd had an emotional affair, because my Heavenly Husband was not first in my life. No wonder I lived in despair. God knew I needed to be broken—for me to see that I was completely contentious, quarrelsome, a bad housewife (after reading *workers@home*), and that I was always making it a point to share my opinion—when I didn't have a clue what God said about anything. As I started taking the courses, along with reading the two books, reading the devotionals, fasting and having alone time with God each morning, while also no longer watching television, I began to seek His face. I asked Him to forgive me and please just love me, because I was not being loved. I know this happened because it was my husband who was the center of my life. Well, honestly, the center of my life was ME.

What principles, from God's Word (or through our resources), Agustina, did the Lord teach you during this trial?

First, I sought the Lord for everything—every need, every question. I knew only He had the answer. Then I stopped arguing; I stopped all my stupid speeches I'd make about everything I knew nothing about. I stopped all social media and pretty much stayed to myself, because I'm too jealous and suspicious, so if I heard anything regarding my husband, I knew I'd fall for the enemy's schemes again. I decided to take better care of my house and my clothes and his, to keep the house tidy. I worked through *workers@home* and found I was asking Him to forgo the career that I once thought was so important but now I hated.

I became more loving towards everyone. I was no longer calling all the time to know where my husband was or what he was doing. I no longer cared if he never came to sleep with me, and I stopped questioning why he no longer wanted to be intimate with me. I no longer craved it; I think because I wanted to feel loved by this act, but I never felt loved at all. I needed His love, so I could give love. I do thank God that my husband didn't leave home, as so many testimonies say happened to them.

So if things got tough, if I saw and heard more than I wanted to, I knew not to complain or whine but to remain thankful that I'd come to my senses, before He needed to allow my husband to leave me in order to get my attention.

What were the most difficult times that God helped you through, Agustina?

The hardest part has been letting go, because he never left, so I needed to not know or care what he was doing on the internet or who I could hear him talking to very late at night. Yes, it was very difficult, but as I became more focused on my HH, it got so much better, until I really had no concern about what he was doing, not at all.

Agustina, what was the "turning point" of your restoration?

I can't pinpoint when things began to turn. It was gradual, as I began to change. Maybe it was after really reading *A Wise Woman,* when I'd determined to build my life on the Rock. Before that, my husband was totally ignoring me, but within a week of reading a WW, he was already talking to me again and was already praising the food I'd prepared (preparing it no longer in haste but just dreaming of being a good wife and pleasing God).

Soon after talking to my HH about being a *worker@home,* without me saying one thing to my husband, he mentioned that he'd heard of a way to make an income at home. He asked if I would consider quitting my job, and he said he would help me find clients to work from home, doing the same thing that I did for the company I was working for.

I know I still have a very long way on my journey, but I believe God wants to restore every area of our lives, and often He does it in the blink of an eye. Our financial life was in ruins, but I no longer worry about the bills, nor do I complain to him anymore. I don't worry about him, or finances or anything else. God has taught me that me telling Him is all I need to do, so I can retain and ooze the gentle and quiet spirit that's so precious to God, and that is what draws a husband back to a wife, too. I am so happy with my Precious Husband, and because I've been so happy and want to be forever His, maybe the turning point is when I told my HH I didn't need anything but Him, and I really meant it.

Tell us HOW it happened, Agustina. Did your husband just walk in the front door? Agustina, did you suspect or could you tell you were close to being restored?

It's hard to say when the restoration actually occurred, because he never left. But it's very clear we are restored, because our life as a couple is brand new. I am not the same, and because of me changing, so has my husband. I don't see him on his computer; he rarely goes out without asking me to come along. Our intimacy is better than ever, because it's based on love not lust.

Would you recommend any of our resources in particular that helped you, Agustina?

I recommend every single thing this ministry offers. Erin has been and will always be the biggest blessing in my life. Where would I be if she did not share what God taught her and if she had not been willing to give her life to helping women like me? I am always showing women *the books* and telling them to visit the site—and to do so before they find themselves in a crisis.

Would you be interested in helping encourage other women, Agustina?

Yes

Either way, Agustina, what kind of encouragement would you like to leave women with, in conclusion?

Dear Bride, simply follow the Lord's principles and believe His promises. Do not give up on your marriage, and don't follow what everyone else says. Only God knows what changes need to be made and if your heart is in the right place.

Do not play into the enemy's schemes. God has given us our families, our husbands. Be part of His army of women around the world who encourage other women to search for the Lord as their Husband. This is the key to restoring so many broken marriages and families. God is by our side, so we cannot fail.

Chapter 20

Bianca

"His own iniquities will capture the wicked,
And he will be held with the cords of his sin."
—Proverbs 5:22

"His Eyes Wide with Both Fear and Wonder"

Bianca, how did your restoration actually begin?

Well, my husband and I married and have been together since we were in our teens. We were both believers and got together often with both our families. But due to our work schedules, focusing on our son (and me looking at men), we drifted apart, and my husband stopped going to church, but I continued going. There was no respect on my part, and we fought a lot, and I was not quiet whatsoever. I answered back with curt comments, when my husband said anything, and I humiliated him, because I felt humiliated.

We worked together (we own our own company), and shouted at each other, and used horrible words in front of our son, so he suffered a lot. I seemed to feel nothing for my husband anymore, and I rejected him whenever he wanted to get close.

I was so tired and sad that I let my son sleep in our bed with me and rejected my husband even more by making him sleep elsewhere. One Sunday, I went to church with my son, and a pastor said my words and actions were hurting my husband and marriage, warning me that I was headed for disaster. I didn't heed the warning that I know now was from God. Finally, my husband couldn't take the rejection anymore, and he was unfaithful. Of course, I was very, very devastated, and I was desperate to stop the horrible pain inside my chest that would not go away.

⌐ried so much that I sought help in the church—help that (at first) helped me a bit. They prayed for me, but my pain would not go away, and I lost a lot of weight and was getting horribly sick. The pastor didn't even know how to help me anymore, and he told me to no longer fast, because I was so weak. I have never suffered so much as I suffered with the pain of this crisis.

Everyone suggested I get help elsewhere (even my pastor), so I went to a psychiatrist to see if he could help me. He had me talk about everything, which only made me feel worse. I left, after he prescribed an antidepressant. I took the prescription and became dangerously ill. The pastor of our church came to pray for me, but I ended up in the hospital, alone and devastated. Then the pastor scheduled me to see their church psychologist, and I went, and I got better temporarily, but then, again, got dangerously worse and was admitted to a psychiatric hospital.

Locked up, I cried all day, and as part of the therapy, we were required to talk to each other. I heard nothing but nonsense or often terrifying accounts of other people's lives, which only intensified my fear and my pain.

I could sense this wasn't what God wanted for me, but I couldn't get out of this pit, this valley of despair. Then one day after I was released, I was on the Internet and began looking for testimonials of restored marriages, because I was desperate to know how other women could overcome this immense pain.

I found the standers sites, but I didn't understand how I could possibly have the energy or desire to "stand" for my marriage or pursue my husband, so I gave up. Then one day, I saw the *book How God Can and Will Restore Your Marriage* on the Internet, and after I purchased it, I was automatically sent to the RMI website. When the book arrived, I read it in two days, and while I was reading, I recognized my mistakes. My husband did not just leave me; it was my contempt for him as a wife that hurt and drove him away.

How did God change your situation, Bianca, as you sought Him wholeheartedly?

I threw myself at His feet and poured out my heart in each course's journal, submitting many reports of praise and jotting down every Word that I was being touched by. I marked my Bible and wept and cried, day after day, fasting and praying and pleading, and all of a sudden my pain turned into joy.

What principles, from God's Word (or through our resources), Bianca, did the Lord teach you during this trial?

Every day, as I read a new lesson, I recognized my mistakes and asked for forgiveness from my HH and also my EH, if the Lord prompted me to do so. Soon, my EH said I was very different, and he even said that to his mother. Thankfully, my heart and anxiousness were quiet, and I did my best not to know about his life away from me anymore, and I stopped listening to others sharing what my EH was doing.

Once I started the courses, I let go of all the counselors. I had already stopped going to the church's psychologist, but I was still asking for prayer because of my despair. But when I learned (after submitting a prayer request) that the Lord wanted me to come to Him, that I didn't need others to pray for me, it was that very day I saw God miraculously act on behalf of me and my family.

I no longer begged my husband to come home, nor asked where he was. I simply asked God to do His best for me, by entrusting everything to Him. I knew I didn't need to beg or plead for His help, but I simply gave Him every concern to work out for my good.

The hardest part was letting go of attending church. After I reached this chapter in my journey, my husband had been a few times, but I wanted more. I wanted a spiritual leader for my son and me. So, by faith, I even let go, and God radically began to transform my EH.

After restoration, it is difficult, and an even deeper relationship is needed. As restored women, we have to be vigilant not to go back to who we were before.

It will be the truth, not what someone else says or feels, that will save you from your pain. It's not even what you believe that you see! Fear not, the Good News is that your heart is safe with Him.

What were the most difficult times that God helped you through, Bianca?

It was very difficult each time I saw that my EH was with the OW. The feeling of injustice, rejection, and contempt wanted to possess me. I would still have felt that way, had I not discovered my own Lover—

my Redeemer and my Husband, Whom I could never take my eyes off of, once I understood and experienced His love for me.

When they came over as a couple, which began to happen more and more often, I would go into my prayer closet to be alone with my HH, to feel His love and hear His loving tender words to me. I would soon feel refreshed and able to entertain my guests with a gentle and quiet spirit.

Bianca, what was the "turning point" of your restoration?

It's when I stopped caring about my own feelings and gave myself into the arms of my HH and began learning, day by day, to fall in love with Him. Once I felt that love, I was able to let go and win my husband without a word using the gentle and quiet spirit that was so wonderful to have and display.

Tell us HOW it happened, Bianca. Did your husband just walk in the front door? Bianca, did you suspect or could you tell you were close to being restored?

It was the Sunday after I got a visit from my former pastor. He came over, because I'd let go of my church. My pastor said it was a mistake, and he told me he didn't believe the husband should be the spiritual leader. The next Sunday, I was at home, having a special Sunday with my HH, and my husband knocked on the door. Each time he'd come by, he would always have the OW, but this time he was alone, and as I let him in, he turned to me and hugged me. I hugged him back, after the shock had quieted in my spirit.

When we sat down, he explained how much he'd tried to come back, but the OW had blackmailed him and stopped him from returning. He told me that when he woke up that morning, he felt free, like the chains or "cords" that were stopping him were gone. I sat there with my mouth wide open, unable to say anything. Then after asking my HH whether I should say something or remain quiet, I said, "Today is the final day of a seven-day fast that I felt led to do. All week there had been two Bible verses that kept coming to mind," and I quoted these two verses to him:

"Is this not the fast which I choose, to loosen the bonds of wickedness, to undo the bands of the yoke, and to let the oppressed go free, and break every yoke?" (Isaiah 58:6).

"His own iniquities will capture the wicked, and he will be held with the cords of his sin" (Proverbs 5:22).

When I'd finished, his mouth was wide open, his eyes wide with both fear and wonder, then tears began filling his eyes and rolling down his cheeks.

Would you recommend any of our resources in particular that helped you, Bianca?

I would recommend every one of your resources to women in this situation or maybe to every woman, so they each could learn these principles and promises. I want to multiply this incredible love I've found, by telling everyone to read through all the *Testimonies* and *books,* and to embrace the teaching in loving the Word of God and having a HH.

Would you be interested in helping encourage other women, Bianca?

Yes, I aim to help and show every woman I meet the true and only Husband we need is Him.

Either way, Bianca, what kind of encouragement would you like to leave women with, in conclusion?

Do not give up on the Lord's promises and truths. Declare and live the Word in your life.

Chapter 21

Tierra

"Husbands, love your wives,
just as Christ also loved the church and
gave Himself up for her, so that He might sanctify her,
having cleansed her by the washing
of water with the word"
—Ephesians 5:25-26

"His Word Washed Away the Guilt and Shame"

Tierra, how did your restoration actually begin?

I was never a person to remember dates, but the day of February 24th is marked forever in my life, because it was the day that God chose to take everything bad that was in my life and show me His power. Several months ago, my marriage was not going well; my husband had changed a lot. I noticed he was depressed, but it was actually due to guilt for committing adultery. Friends and colleagues who knew what was going on told him that if he did not tell me, someone would and that would be worse. So, he decided to tell me and leave the house, because according to him the shame was so much that he could not look at me or our son. He said he needed to get himself straightened out and, when he was better, he would come back.

It was 5 months of not seeing him, along with coldness when we needed to talk, that shocked me into finding hope. He was not the same man I once loved. But this opened the door to meet a new man, the Man of my dreams.

How did God change your situation, Tierra, as you sought Him wholeheartedly?

On the day he left, I felt a hole open beneath my feet, trying to swallow me. But I felt a certain relief, because now I knew why my husband was so different. The first day was very strange, as if it were a nightmare, but after the second day it became hopeless; my son and I would cry in each others' arms. The pain was so much, I could not eat or drink; for many days I did not eat, and as a result, I lost 13kg (28 lbs) in less than 2 months. But the most surprising thing was that I could only think about and talk to God. I prayed all the time, fasted, and sought help on the internet. That's when my life changed. God began showing me that I'd lacked wisdom, so when I searched I found the book *A Wise Woman* on Amazon. Immediately reading just the first few pages, I realized how foolish I was, that I did not take care of my home; I'd pulled it down with my own hands! I made room for the enemy to come in and steal from me, to destroy my life, my son's life, my husband's life.

At that moment, I asked God to forgive me, and I asked Him to change me, because I did not want to be that same woman anymore. I asked Him to teach me how to be the wise woman He wanted me to be. And so my journey began. I discovered your HopeAtLast.com website and began taking the courses, being fed spiritually, feeling stronger than I'd ever felt in my life.

What principles, from God's Word (or through our resources), Tierra, did the Lord teach you during this trial?

Through the book *How God Can and Will Restore Your Marriage*, I began to truly know the Word of God, because every teaching in the book was one Bible verse after the other. I was being "washed with the water of the Word," and it soothed every part of me. It seemed that the book had been written for me; all I had to do was insert my name.

Each day, I began with praise, with singing a love song, and put into practice everything I learned based on the Word of God. This wasn't anyone's opinion; it was what God said but what I'd been ignorant of. First, I let my husband go and learned to seek God with all my heart for every decision I made.

The days and months passed, and I began to feel stronger. I began eating again and to smile, because in my heart there was Someone who loved me—loved me unconditionally. I also knew God would restore my marriage, though I did not know when it would be. I knew it would happen, so it was easy to leave it to God to restore, while I focused on my new Love relationship with my Heavenly Husband.

What were the most difficult times that God helped you through, Tierra?

The most painful moments were when I needed to talk to my husband or receive an email response, as well as the distancing of our son, who at the time was a young adult, so he understood, and therefore felt, the whole situation very much. The coldness in his words chilled me to the bone, because I did not recognize him as the loving caring man he'd always been, not just to me, but to everyone.

In the early days, my prayers had no words, only tears, but I knew that God would harvest each one of them, keeping them in a bottle (Psalm 56:8), and that no matter what difficulty I was going through, He was using it for my good. The tears washed bitterness from my heart, and His Word washed away the guilt and shame I'd lived with since I was a young girl. I was being given a makeover; my Beloved was treating me to a spiritual spa and healing me from the inside out.

Tierra, what was the "turning point" of your restoration?

There wasn't one turning point, but several that changed my life. The first was when I gave up fighting in my strength and gave my battle into God's hand (Exodus 14:13). That's when I asked for His will to be done and not mine. When I could say this to people who inquired what was going on and I was willing to accept the will of God in my heart, I knew I would be fine, regardless of the outcome.

My greatest turning point was becoming His bride; this is when I was fully able to rest and enjoy my life, like never before. Ultimately, it is also what led to my restoration.

Tell us HOW it happened, Tierra. Did your husband just walk in the front door? Tierra, did you suspect or could you tell you were close to being restored?

One day, I drove by a small church near my house (one I'd seen dozens of times) and felt led to go in. As I was sitting, speaking to my Husband, the preacher came up and told me that my husband was there that afternoon! He told me he'd come to confess and get himself right with God.

That night when I got home, I began telling my son what had happened, and my son said, "Mom, Dad put the picture of us back on Facebook," and he'd messaged him asking about it. Our son asked him about that picture, and his dad said he wanted his family back. That same night, he called me, just to talk, but never mentioned anything about going to church or the messaging with our son.

The next day, we did not talk. On Saturday, as I was singing my love song, the phone rang, and it was my husband inviting me to lunch. It was the first time in five months that his voice was calm and composed. I accepted the invitation, and after lunch, as we walked along the river, he apologized for everything he had done and asked if I could ever forgive him, because he was ready to come home. I smiled and said, "Of course," and he seemed very relieved. I said, "Didn't you think I would?" and his answer surprised me. He said, "I thought you might, but I wasn't sure if you'd want me back. I knew you'd met someone. Everyone's been talking about how happy you are, how beautiful you look, so I was hopeful but prepared for you to say no."

So we sat down, and I was able to tell him about my relationship with my Heavenly Husband and how it had healed me. He didn't say much at that time, but I could see he was listening, trying his best to understand.

What surprised me was that he already had his luggage in the car to return home, so that's where we went, home.

Like Erin says, the next few days were not easy. Both he and I were apprehensive of what it would be like to be living as husband and wife again. His biggest fear, he told me later, was not getting my trust back, and he was also struggling with accusations I'd made about him in the past. I feared the possibility of not trusting, or being cheated on, as I'd been in the past.

Yet, each time when my mind was filled with evil thoughts, of fears about my husband or my restoration, I would run and find my way to a quiet place to talk to my Beloved Husband. I would ask Him about each concern, and each time He would replace the lie with the truth. This pattern started long before my restoration, so I had practiced it so much that it was instinctive after restoration.

My husband soon began feeling more comfortable, and I can see him every day living in a way that makes me happy to see. We just received our Couple's Packet, and we have set this weekend to begin studying the workbooks together.

Would you recommend any of our resources in particular that helped you, Tierra?

I recommend all the materials from your bookstore and the online courses to everyone I know! I am very happy to have the gift of the couple's book for my husband now. Thank you partners. I have already given away many of your books to the many women I know, because after what happened to us, I run into so many with difficulty in marriage that need these books.

Would you be interested in helping encourage other women, Tierra?

Yes

Either way, Tierra, what kind of encouragement would you like to leave women with, in conclusion?

Women who go through some difficulty in marriage must first seek God, and from there God will direct them to the relationship with their HH that will change everything. In addition, we each lack wisdom, so learning to be Wise Women and Wise Men will help change the course of so many lives that are intertwined with ours.

Do not be carried away by what the world preaches (and many churches also preach). It's a lie that God accepts divorce; it's a lie that once betrayed, the sinner will betray again. Trust in the God you serve, not in what the the world speaks. We are told to trust Him and no one else. And when we do, He is faithful.

"Cursed is the man who trusts in mankind and makes flesh his strength..."

"Blessed is the man who trusts the Lord." Jer. 17:5, 7.

Chapter 22

Bridgette

"For on account of a harlot one is reduced to a loaf of bread,
And an adulteress hunts for the precious life."
—Proverbs 6:26

"Get Out!! Never Speak to Me Again!!"

Bridgette, how did your restoration actually begin?

Dear friends who are traveling this same journey, I've come to share my restored marriage testimony, to the Honor and Glory of my Beloved Lord.

We had just celebrated 15 years of marriage and were expecting our first, long-hoped-for daughter. We were both very happy with the arrival of the baby, but I had complications in the last months of pregnancy, and I believe that's when I began my journey.

I was always overweight in our marriage, and my husband always demanded that I take more care and always blamed my weight on our lack of intimacy. He was okay with it, but I tended to avoid intimacy, due to the shame of being overweight.

When my daughter was born, I was hospitalized close to 3 weeks. Remaining in the hospital, for some reason, led to me becoming very contentious and demanding. I never realized I'd been harboring a lot of anger in my heart, and I'd forgotten that my Lord even existed. To top it all, I no longer was grateful for the good things that happened—like finally being able to conceive and being blessed by a healthy baby girl.

I became a demanding, irate person, because I wanted to run the house my way! I did not like his family to stay in our house for a long time, even though they came to help. When I remember how selfish and bitter I was, I am so ashamed.

After my daughter turned a year, I noticed my husband was different. He was cold, distracted, and we seemed to fight about everything.

Slowly, he began to want space, time and freedom from me, and he began going out alone with friends.

One day, I couldn't stand it. I was angry, so I stood with my hands on my hips, got in his face and said, "Is there something you want to tell me?" He almost shouted, "Yes!! I don't love you anymore; I'm still young, and I want to be happy, and I'm sorry, but I found another woman who makes me very happy!"

At that moment, my world collapsed, and since I didn't know how to act in a situation like this (something I was totally unprepared for and never thought in a million years would happen), I shoved him and yelled, "Get out!! Just go pack your things and never speak to me again!!" That night, he went to his sister's house, but later, I discovered that he stayed for just one night, then he went to live with OW.

How did God change your situation, Bridgette, as you sought Him wholeheartedly?

After my husband left, I lost weight very fast. I think I heard Chelle calling it the "infidelity diet." I could not eat or sleep, nor take care of my daughter. I was in deep depression. Something in my heart cried for the restoration of my family, even without knowing how it could possibly work. I went to speak to my husband several times and asked him to come back, but that only increased the wall of hate that was impenetrable. I cried every day, and for a long time I did not seek the Lord. At one point, when I was at my lowest, I fell to the floor and begged God for forgiveness for leaving Him.

Soon after, I found myself searching the internet about divorce and reconciliation. I found several websites, but none gave me hope. Then, a few months later, by the mercy of the Lord, I found RMI. I got the book *How God Can and Will Restore Your Marriage,* and when I read it, I was reluctant to believe that I had really torn down my house with my own hands. But the more I sat alone listening to God speak to me, the more I knew I really had done this.

I started devouring the book, and then I took the FREE course. I started to change my attitude and stopped listening to other people telling me to divorce my husband. I saw first hand the power of fasting and prayer, because I had never fasted before, but I saw things happen during those days that I never dreamed were possible. In the midst of almost every fast, often on the third day, my husband would often show up at our home to visit my daughter, and when he came, due to being so weak from fasting, I was kind and gentle to him—a different spirit than the one he'd seen in me before.

What principles, from God's Word (or through our resources), Bridgette, did the Lord teach you during this trial?

I started applying each of the principles, as I read the RMI materials and intensely studied the Bible, looking up every verse I read. The principle of letting go was probably the most important and the most difficult. When I went looking for my husband, he would try to get away from me. But when I searched for my HH and His love, then suddenly my husband would come around looking for me.

One of the most difficult times was when he first came home (my first restoration) and left three days later, when the OW (other woman) sent a message asking him to return. I had to start over again, because in dreams and in my heart, the Lord told me it wasn't over; there was a bigger battle left to be fought.

Another difficult time was when my earthly husband began to go into depression, due to his financial situation. But I knew why it was happening and just kept quiet. Just as the Word of the Lord says, "For on account of a harlot one is reduced to a loaf of bread, and an adulteress hunts for the precious life. Can a man take fire to his bosom, and his clothes not be burned? The one who commits adultery with a woman is lacking sense; he who would destroy himself does it. Wounds and disgrace he will find, and his reproach will not be blotted out" (Prov. 6:24–33).

One day, he called to talk to me and said I was the only person he trusted, and he told me who the OW was and how she told him to leave her alone, because he was also involved with someone else. He said he had nowhere to go, so he was living at his sister's house again. I knew how easily I could say, "come back home," but it had to be at the appointed time. I suffered a lot from seeing his life like that, and that's when the Lord told me to stop praying for my EH, to allow him to suffer enough to want his life to change. So I did.

Bridgette, what was the "turning point" of your restoration?

The turning point was when he started coming home and seeing all the dramatic changes my HH was making in me—both physical and how I was behaving. I was very aloof, because I had a Lover, and I could see that was drawing him back, like alluring him when I wasn't trying to.

When he first asked to sleep at home, I knew not to deny intimacy with him, which later he said helped him to want to return home.

Tell us HOW it happened, Bridgette. Did your husband just walk in the front door? Bridgette, did you suspect, or could you tell you were close to being restored?

He was constantly coming home, sleeping here, and then returning to his sister's house. Gradually, I noticed that he was bringing his clothes home, making plans for the future, and one day, I realized he'd been home for weeks. That's when I asked my HH if I was restored, and He answered, "It is finished," and reminded me that I owed Him praise and to fill out my restoration form.

Would you recommend any of our resources in particular that helped you, Bridgette?

Yes, I would recommend all your resources; each one has helped me a lot. I read and reread the book *How God Can and Will Restore Your Marriage* and *A Wise Woman* paperbacks, marking them and writing in the margins. But I found most of the help in the online courses and by journaling.

Would you be interested in helping encourage other women, Bridgette?

Yes

Either way, Bridgette, what kind of encouragement would you like to leave women with, in conclusion?

Don't give up. Even though you think it's impossible (just as I thought), hold on to the Lord with both hands! Seek His Word for all your answers. And when you think nothing is happening, trust me, you're wrong! God never sleeps, and the Lord is busy working on your behalf, when you focus on loving Him. We don't need to see what He's doing; we just need to believe.

UPDATE: I wanted to add to my RMT. There's another situation that I'd like to share to encourage the women reading my testimony. My husband had been home for more than 6 months, when he became cold and distant again. In those first few months, I faced rejection and a variety of other trials. Several times, I thought about giving up, but thought, "why?" God is who restored my marriage, so He will be the One to complete it. I chose instead to begin a rendezvous with the Lover of my Soul, and I remained lovesick for our beloved Lord. Just as it says, "when the battle is the Lord's, the victory is ours," that is exactly what happened. In a single day, everything changed, and our marriage in now better than it has ever been!!

So dear friends, don't strive to restore or keep your marriage restored. You'll be tested, believe me, and the test is where your heart is. Keep it His; it is difficult, once your husband is home, but be diligent to make time for your First Love (I make lunch dates with Him, alone in the park, or my car when it's raining.) Do what you have to, but don't go back.

Chapter 23

Cadence

"Therefore the Lord longs to be gracious to you,
And therefore He waits on high to have
compassion on you."
—Isaiah 30:18

"He Was Silent and He Began to Weep"

Cadence, how did your restoration actually begin?

Dear friends, my journey began about a year ago, when my husband and I began to have daily disagreements, but by the end of the day we were fine. Even at the time, I saw it as foolish disagreements, because I did not understand what I did that irritated him so much, and meanwhile, my husband was increasing his anger toward me day after day.

One day when I left work, I found a cell phone in the back of the car, and when I asked whose it was, my husband said he had given a ride to some friends of the company he worked for. I was very restless, and at the first opportunity I searched the cell phone, and what I found did not make me happy—because there were messages from my husband to a woman on that phone!! I was speechless; I fell to my knees in despair!

My foolish attitude took over, and I filed for divorce against my husband. I blatantly told everyone that I no longer trusted him, that, yes, I loved him, but that I no longer trusted him.

Beloved, I did this to my husband in order to punish him, because what I had discovered was serious, so I showed the phone to him, when I got back from my attorney. At the time, I thought it was not right to act as if nothing had happened, not let him get away with it, so my only recourse was to file for a divorce.

At first my husband was reluctant, but I pretended to be firm. Our marriage could not withstand the ongoing fights that led to us becoming farther and farther apart from one another. I knew that, but then one day, he suddenly told me that he no longer loved me and he wanted the divorce.

I fell into much deeper despair and changed course. I began to chase after my husband with text messages and phone messages where I would cry and beg him to love me again. I humiliated myself day after day, but he was adamant about his decision. He packed and left home, hoping to distance himself from me.

I prayed for my marriage every day, but I prayed wrong. I was distressed; I was asking God, "What have I done?" Nothing. "Why was my husband treating me that way, because I didn't deserve it?" This all was very painful, so I just heard what I wanted to hear.

After a few days, I went to a prayer meeting at my sister's house, hoping to find something to hang onto. While there, God "gave me a word" from a woman who came to the meeting. She told me that my marriage was not God's will, but then I remembered the Word of God, and I told my sister quietly that I didn't believe that woman, because God's Word isn't discouraging. My sister said, "I agree; God restores marriages!" Praise God!!!! The word that, "God restores marriages" ran over and over in my mind, and when I lay down that night to sleep, I felt led to get back up and search Google for "Marriages Restored by God," and that's when my journey began! I found RMI!!!!

I read several testimonies, and each pointed to this ministry. I ordered Erin's book, *How God Can and Will Restore Your Marriage,* and then filled out the Marriage Evaluation at HopeAtLast.com, immediately getting an Evaluation offering me FREE courses.

I followed each lesson step-by-step. It was hard. I realized I was wrong so many times, but God in His infinite mercy comforted me and gave me chances upon chances to do the lessons over, until I got it right.

I actually asked God to show me my mistakes, and it was amazing, because He showed them to me one by one, so I could be healed from them all. I saw how much bitterness was in me and that I was as guilty as my husband had been. I realized that I had allowed the enemy into my life to use my ignorance and lack of knowing His Word to destroy me and our marriage.

God opened my eyes and took care of me; He taught me to pray, to truly love Him, to seek Him for every answer, to fast, to be obedient and to forgive.

The more I prayed, the more my husband moved away. It seemed that restoration would be impossible. My husband went out with other women, got serious with one, but he hid her and their relationship from me. Praise God.

Today, I want to shout to the Honor and Glory of the Lord that GOD restored my Marriage! To God be given all Honor and All Glory!

How did God change your situation, Cadence, as you sought Him wholeheartedly?

God changed my situation, as I sought Him with all my heart, when I took my eyes off my husband, when I let go. The more I exhibited a gentle and quiet spirit, the more "the contentious woman" died and was gone, the more I won my husband without a word, the less impossible I could sense my marriage was becoming. However, there were no signs, no improvement whatsoever. Instead, it was trust and what was unseen that led to restoration.

I stopped looking at my situation (that was getting worse) and looked only at what God could do, which was the impossible; that is when I stopped looking at my husband's mistakes and was given an opportunity to ask forgiveness for my mistakes. When I wanted my Heavenly Husband more than I wanted my marriage, I got closer to restoration.

I asked God to mold me, to transform me, to restore me to my HH. As a result, He gave me all of that and also my husband, and my marriage!! Only God could do that!!

What principles, from God's Word (or through our resources), Cadence, did the Lord teach you during this trial?

Letting my husband go, looking to God and not considering my deteriorating situation was most important...to forgive, to obey, and to want HIM above all things.

What were the most difficult times that God helped you through, Cadence?

There was a day that my husband went to take me to work, and on the way he told me that he wanted to sell our home, because it made no sense for him to stay in a property with me—because he needed to buy himself something new where he could live alone. At that moment, I spoke to my HH, asking Him to suppress the tears that were coming, and that's when my husband said we would talk about it later. We were on our way to church, so when we arrived for the service, I went to the bathroom where I was able to cry out to God. I spent the whole morning saying: "Darling, HH, I trust You!"

At the time, I had the desire to buy my husband's part of our home in order to keep it, but when I spoke to my HH, He told me not to stand in the way of what my husband wanted to do. So the next time he brought it up, I immediately agreed with him, putting on a big smile (trusting Him), and I said, if he wanted to, we could go ahead and put it up for sale.

Beloved, I saw the miracle of God before me—my husband was silent, and he began to weep. My husband could not say a word. God turned his heart immediately, because I trusted and obeyed Him. When my husband stopped crying, he began shaking his head, denying that he wanted to sell.

Cadence, what was the "turning point" of your restoration?

The turning point was when I wanted my HH more than my husband or marriage.

Tell us HOW it happened, Cadence. Did your husband just walk in the front door? Cadence, did you suspect, or could you tell you were close to being restored?

My husband never fully left me. He kept in touch, called and was always willing to help me. But at first, he was a bit gruff and sure in his decision to divorce. There was a short period when he seemed to hate me, but little by little God took the hate wall down. The more I fell in love with my HH, the more my husband came closer and closer to me. The more often he called, the more he wanted to see me, and said that he missed me.

An interesting thing: I always asked God in my prayers to remove every bad thought that my earthly husband had about me and replace it with never being able to forget me, no matter what he was doing. God did more than that, because my husband reported that he couldn't get me out of his mind, he said that once he saw a woman holding her hair away from her face, and it reminded him of the way I held it.

The day my restoration happened, I was working, and my husband sent me a very long message, saying that wanting to divorce me was the biggest mistake in his life and the big mistake before that was when he had separated from me. He said that I had changed, that I was a better person, and that he still loved me, maybe more now than ever. That day, he moved back home.

Would you recommend any of our resources in particular that helped you, Cadence?

I recommend all materials!

Would you be interested in helping encourage other women, Cadence?

Yes!

Either way, Cadence, what kind of encouragement would you like to leave women with, in conclusion?

Don't give up on your marriage! Don't give up on your family! This happened for a GOOD reason. The reason was to change you, to help you find your HH and His love. Simply pray, fast and seek God with all your heart! Believe in the miracle He just longs to give you!

Chapter 24

Aurora

"Now to him who is able to do
immeasurably more than all we ask or imagine,
according to his power that is at work within us..."
—Ephesians 3:20

"He Called Me to Pick Him Up"

Aurora, how did your restoration actually begin?

It's been two months since my husband returned home! I had not yet begun journalling the RMI courses, when he returned, because I had been given the *How God Can and Will Restore Your Marriage* book 3 months prior to his return, and only when he returned did I realize there were FREE online courses. I already had in my heart that there should be no divorce and that I should believe God for my marriage, but I didn't know where to start. Today, while doing one of the C2 (Rebuilding Your Life) lessons, I felt the need to submit my testimony and give God the praise He deserves.

It all started about eight months ago, when I suspected my husband had gone out with an OW. After months of fights, arguments, a lot of crying and distrust (my distrust of my EH, of course), he decided to leave home. He went to a friend's house and said he wasn't with anyone. He never totally left me; he called me every day, showed up at home several times a week, but he said he wouldn't come back, that our marriage wasn't working anymore. In the end, after he moved back home, I found that he was involved with the OW. That motivated me to complete the courses and begin to relate to the Lord as my Heavenly Husband.

How did God change your situation, Aurora, as you sought Him wholeheartedly?

God had touched my heart before being given the RYM book by a friend, so I was already praying and asking Him to bring my husband back. But when I started reading *How God Can and Will Restore Your Marriage*, I was sure I was on the right track. What's more, I could see how much I was responsible for the downfall of my marriage.

So often, I begin to remember the things I did, the situations that happened, and I can't believe how foolish I was. God is changing me every day, and He is shaping me according to His will. I was always a very selfish person; I wanted to be right about everything; sometimes I even let things go, but inside I didn't accept what anyone said. I was extremely bossy, jealous, angry and a completely bitter person. God took it all from me. Glory to God! I became a calmer, quieter and less anxious person—a gentle and quiet woman. I was able to forgive my husband, and what I think is the most important thing: I could see my sins, and in addition to asking forgiveness from God, I also asked forgiveness from my husband, because he was one of the people most harmed by them.

What principles, from God's Word (or through our resources), Aurora, did the Lord teach you during this trial?

I learned that we should love our HH and that He must be in the first place: He must be first in our lives, in every way, for He gives us everything we need according to His will and His abundance.

What were the most difficult times that God helped you through, Aurora?

When I learned that there really was a relationship with my husband and the OW, it was very difficult, but with the Lord's help (especially after He became my HH after reading the Abundant Life courses), I managed not to let it get me down.

Today, even though he is at home and he is no longer involved with the OW—trials continue to come into my life. In some ways, they're even harder, but He has sustained me at all times. Whenever I need Him, I simply whisper to Him, "My Love, I need Your help," and immediately He lifts me up!

Aurora, what was the "turning point" of your restoration?

I cannot say exactly what the turning point of my restoration was, but when I clung to the Lord and cried to Him, I could tell that everything got easier!

Tell us HOW it happened, Aurora. Did your husband just walk in the front door? Aurora, did you suspect or could you tell you were close to being restored?

The day I heard about his relationship with the OW, he'd called, so I asked him if it was true (I still didn't know the principle of being quiet :)). He told me that he was glad I knew (it was through another person hearing it on social media and telling me), because he was finished, done with her. He said he was already planning to come home, to talk to me about moving home. If I was interested in having this conversation, he would come home the next day. He did come, but his heart was turned away from me again. He said he had changed his mind, that "we" wouldn't work, and I was supposed to give him up, let him go. I agreed with him. I would let him go and give up. (I'd just read to agree with your adversary, and parts of doing it enthusiastically, when I got to the Facing Divorce Again course).

Anyway, twelve days later, he called me before dawn, asking me to pick him up because he wanted to talk. It was early on Saturday, and by Sunday night, he was already home, moved back in. Glory to God!

It has not been an easy battle (God battling for me and my battle in my mind), because the enemy has tried every way to make him leave again, but I have remained steadfast in prayer and agreeing with anything he says, with a big smile, while speaking to my HH for His will to be done.

Would you recommend any of our resources in particular that helped you, Aurora?

I recommend all your materials: books, devotionals, testimonies, and daily encouragement. Sometimes, when I am a little discouraged, and I see a Saturday restored marriage testimony, it reminds me of a lesson and promise I need. I can then remember that for God all things are possible and that I should not be led by my thoughts, but I should focus on God's plans and His promises whenever the enemy is trying to bring me down.

I really appreciate everyone here at RMI. It's because of what you do that women like me are helped! May God continue to bless you all!

Would you be interested in helping encourage other women, Aurora?

Yes for sure!!

Either way, Aurora, what kind of encouragement would you like to leave women with, in conclusion?

Fellow brides, don't give up! With God anything is possible, and He will do wonders in your life. When you are discouraged, read Psalm 46:10 "Be still and know that I am God; I will be exalted among the Gentiles and I will be exalted upon the earth," and remember that "God is able to do infinitely more than we ask and we think" (Ephesians 3:20).

This is what we need to do: "Ask, and it shall be given you; seek, and ye shall find; knock, and it shall be opened unto you" (Matthew 7:7), and "Fear not; believe only" (Mark 5:36).

Beloved, may the peace of the Lord be with you all.

Chapter 25

Valeria

"The man who had died came forth,
bound hand and foot with wrappings,
and his face was wrapped around with a cloth.
Jesus said to them, 'Unbind him, and let him go.'"
—John 11:44

"He Returned Home without Anything and Never Looked Back!!"

Valeria, how did your restoration actually begin?

It all started after several attempts to file for a divorce and each time God would stop me. Every time I tried, something would stop it from happening. Then one day, I ran into my husband and that's when I realized, "I'm fighting with God"! When I got home I said to Him, "Lord, why didn't you stop me from seeing him?" (When my EH saw me at the registry, he came to give me a hug and I turned my face away from him, I didn't hug him and I couldn't look at his face). And then the Lord said, "I allowed you to go there to see what was in your heart. Your heart is full of hatred, self-pity, unforgiveness, and resentment." I asked the Lord, "Lord, how can I forgive him for all that he did to me?" And He answered me, "Ask me, every day, every time you feel hurt or angry." This is when my personal restoration began.

God began to do amazing things to me. First, I had to take the log out of my own eye, I had to ask for forgiveness for my own sins. Every day I asked the Lord to help me forgive my EH. After about four months my EH came to me (let me say that this was a huge breakthrough because he never wished me a "Merry Christmas", "Happy New Year", he had said nothing to me for months!) But once I let go completely, as soon as I had not wanted to know anything about what he was doing anymore, when I stopped poking around in his life it came with so many blessings.

But right away the enemy came to steal my joy when I found out that he had bought a piece of land from the OW, but that day the Lord spoke to me saying that I had to stop fussing and I couldn't complain anymore because He proved that He was in control. I stopped complaining but the enemy continued to torment my mind with remembering things that were said and different situations that happened. Each time it was pushing me to find out more about the OW. I was so tempted to send him an email but the next day I did as the course teaches us, I wrote an email but in the end: "I sent it to myself."

After I passed this test, the hate-wall fell. And during this "process" of "letting go" I was able to check off my prayer journal all the things I asked the Lord to do for me. Things like renewing my mind, forgiving and being forgiven.

It took four months from that sad day of the "failed divorce"(glory to God) when he came to me. At first he came to me about something he needed me to fix in an email. Even though the first meeting was uneventful, before he left he asked me to pray for him and from then on, we started a friendship. But since he was already living with OW by this time, he could only call me and we would exchange a lot of emails and that's how our friendship grew and grew. Soon he started talking about coming back. Next he said he was coming back but we needed to "fix" a situation first.

How did God change your situation, Valeria, as you sought Him wholeheartedly?

As I said, when he started saying he wanted to come back, I started to face new and more difficult battles. Battles in my mind, temptations to go against what I'd learned. Because he started saying he was coming back near my birthday, each month began to pass: May, June, July, August, and September. And each time the enemy tormented me, reminding me of similar situations when he decided to leave the house and he said he was coming back but it never happened. And so I had to start reading more and more of God's Word, the book *How God Can and Will Restore Your Marriage* over and over again to arm me with faith, the full armor of God.

What principles, from God's Word (or through our resources), Valeria, did the Lord teach you during this trial?

The key principle of letting go. The principle of reading and meditating on God's Word day and night. The principle of asking no one, but only seeking God's direction and "telling Him" everything before calling a friend. The principle of forgiveness, which brings healing. The principle of removing the log from my eye and that who accuses is the enemy. The Pharisee hypocritical spirit principle I had. The principle of beginning to empty myself then filling myself with the Word of God. The principle of stating my HH was all I wanted, needed, and cared for.

What were the most difficult times that God helped you through, Valeria?

There were so many. I would wake up screaming in the middle of the night. Once I was screaming into my pillow to stifle the screams. I needed to scream because I felt like I was suffocating. The other was the hate-wall that I created, but I'm so glad I discovered what Psalm 88:8 says (that God has taken my husband away from me) so it no longer hurt.

Valeria, what was the "turning point" of your restoration?

The turning point was when God totally turned my husband's heart back toward me, even though he said he could not leave the OW.

Tell us HOW it happened, Valeria? Did your husband just walk in the front door? Valeria, did you suspect or could you tell you were close to being restored?

I was already aware that God had restored my marriage because of the passionate emails we exchanged, but I couldn't understand why he didn't leave the OW's house and come back to live with me. Then one day He led me to the passage of Lazarus' resurrection (again)—I already knew the passage and opened it to the part when it said, "take away the stone" because He used that to show me my unforgiveness. But He led me to read and reread and reread it again to understand why he didn't leave the house of OW and I realized that after Jesus sent Lazarus to get up, He says Lazarus' feet and hands were tied and there is a handkerchief over his eyes. I realized God turned his heart, but He still needed to remove the blindness from his eyes regarding the OW who wouldn't let him leave her and return to me.

Many trials came to test my faith and produce patience, so I fought back by repeating this verse in my head and heart, that it was happening for me to produce patience and the work would be complete!

In the meantime, I had learned to thank my HH for everything and to praise Him, to seek Him only. I went back to watching the Be

Encouraged eVideos and in one of them, Erin tells the story of Asa's. And, carelessly, reading testimonies of another ministry (big mistake) I called my pastor to talk. I wrongly believed we need to talk and listen to someone, which now I do NOT recommend, as Erin teaches us, because the Bible says He is our Wonderful Counselor.

At this point, I hadn't let go of attending church, thinking it didn't apply to me, so when I didn't get the answers I wanted from God, off I went to talk to the pastor. This was my last time I stepped foot in a church. I never went again but finally letting go. My eyes were opened when this very polite and kind shepherd actually scolded me for having "friendship" with my husband! Telling me I should move on, let the OW have him and find myself my own good, godly man!!

I prayed all night begging God for forgiveness and for going to that pastor who told me what was contrary to what I was learning at RMI, what the Bible said. The pastor told me that it was foolish to be gentle, to speak kindly, every time I had the opportunity to talk to my husband. Again the Lord reminded me of Erin speaking of Asa, so I went to read in my Bible and when it opened, it opened in this passage and I realized that the Lord would not finish the good work because I wanted approval from the pastor. But because the Lord directed me here, to RMI, and He was already taking care of me, that I finally needed to let go of my church and stop thinking I could pick and choose the principles I wanted to follow. Glory to God for that.

I want to make it clear that this pastor's ministry is good, but you must stay where God first directed you because He knows all things. And from the beginning, I was directed to the RMI site and it was here that I found the answers to many questions I'd asked Him. I had learned to "arm myself" with the written verses, the Sword that is the Word of God. And with that answer, I came to love Him even more and to thank Him for EVERYTHING.

I began singing LOVE Songs and let go of Christian music. Glory to God, He continued to take care of me! Just before restoration, I nearly suffered two car accidents and in both of them I survived a "near miss" but each time, still shaking, I would begin to praise Him and thank Him! After the second one, I turned on the radio and "our song" was playing!

After a year and a half apart, I left the building where I live to get a coffee and when I looked up, there was my husband and he was walking towards me smiling. That day my husband came home. He returned home to me walking (he'd lost his car), without any of his clothes or any of his belongings. Without asking anything, he settled into his home with me, bought some new clothes and never looked back!!

Would you recommend any of our resources in particular that helped you, Valeria?

For sure! Absolutely *How God Can and Will Restore Your Marriage*, the *Be Encouraged eVideos* (they were really great!), and without a doubt the courses and to be sure to journal. Each of your free resources have been very important, it seems like everything was written for me. I also recommend God's Word, we must read it and meditate day and night as the Psalmist teaches us. And before your husband gets home be sure you've gone through *A Wise Woman* at least twice so you're prepared.

Would you be interested in helping encourage other women, Valeria?

Yes

Either way, Valeria, what kind of encouragement would you like to leave women with, in conclusion?

I'd like to leave you with His Word.

"Do not be afraid; You will not suffer shame. Do not fear embarrassment; You will not be humiliated. You will forget the shame of your youth and you will no longer remember the humiliation of your widowhood. For her Maker is her husband, the Lord of hosts is her name, the Holy One of Israel is her Redeemer; He is called the God of all the earth. The Lord will call you back as if you were an abandoned and grieving woman, a woman who was married again only to be rejected," says her God. "For a brief moment I left her, but with deep compassion I will bring her back. In an impulse of indignation I hid my face from you for a moment, but with everlasting kindness I will have compassion on you," says the Lord your Redeemer. Isaiah 54:4-8 NIV

"When the Lord brought the captives back to Zion, it was like a dream. Then our mouth was filled with laughter and our tongue with songs of joy." Psalm 126:1-2 NIV

"Without faith it is impossible to please God." Hebrews 11:6 NIV.

"Delight yourself in the Lord, and he will answer the desires of your heart." Psalm 37:4 NIV

"My brethren, consider it a joy to go through many trials, for you know that the test of your faith produces perseverance. And perseverance must take complete action, that you may be mature and whole, without lacking anything to you." James 1: 2-4 NIV

"The king's heart is like a river controlled by the Lord; he drives him wherever he wants." Proverbs 21:1 NIV

After saying this, Jesus shouted aloud, "Lazarus, come out!" The dead man came out, his hands and feet wrapped in linen strips and his face wrapped in cloth. Jesus said to them, "Take off his sashes and let him go." John 11:43-44 NIV

"Love forgives many sins." 1 Peter 4:8 NIV

"Support one another and forgive any complaints you have against each other. Forgive as the Lord has forgiven you. But above all, put on love, which is the perfect link." Colossians 3:13-14 NIV

Chapter 26

Alice

"A constant dripping on a day of steady rain
And a contentious woman are alike."
—Proverbs 27:15

"Please Make Me a New Woman"

Alice, how did your restoration actually begin?

Good morning beloved brides! I've missed all of you. I haven't submitted anything for quite some time and felt convicted. I want to help other women, but I often find myself disappearing because I feel limited in my abilities and I didn't know how to help. I'm so thankful I returned and see FB ministries giving me a way to help.

I came to this ministry desperate because I had tried finding help with several pastors, went to a women's retreat on marriage, but got no good answers about my marriage situation.

My husband left home in May about four years before finding RMI. We had a discussion that turned nasty, which was the last straw for both of us. We lived for fighting, we had no peace in our home and I lived in a deep depression. He was either away or spending all his time on the Internet when he was home. He began adding a bunch of weird women to his facebook. I didn't understand what was going on and no matter how hard I tried I couldn't change it. I complained all the time that he no longer read the Bible nor prayed. I saw his faith slipping through his hands and could do nothing. Now I know it's because only He, our dearly Beloved, could do it. But at the time I was a Pharisee and I thought I was very Holy and anointed. It annoyed my EH even more because I was far from Holy, I was contentious and annoying, manipulative and how no clue what the truth but that didn't stop me from preaching at everyone.

We actually had a messed up relationship since we first met. But God has been good to us in our lives, love has always been present despite so much turmoil. The reason he turned away from me and tried to talk to other women was the way I treated him, always harsh and defensive. It did not follow the word of God and I was nothing but constant dripping, a contentious woman.

How did God change your situation, Alice, as you sought Him wholeheartedly?

When I discovered the RMI website I had hope for the first time, I found what I was looking for and couldn't find anywhere else. I was hungry for God, I read the daily praise reports, all the books, and I meditated on the Word. God changed me when I recognized how unbearable I was to live with and asked my Husband to please make me a new woman. That's when I felt Him so close to me that I could hear His voice talking to me.

What principles, from God's Word (or through our resources), Alice, did the Lord teach you during this trial?

I learned to wait and rest in Him, for without Him we are nothing and we can do nothing. I was always very anxious and had to obsess about everything I didn't think was perfect, not in myself but in everyone else. I learned to forgive, I thought I would never be able to forgive him for abandoning me and getting involved with other women. But when I did I was set free to love.

I learned to humble myself and ask forgiveness in the midst of this whole situation, I forgave others and forgave my husband, but first asking God to forgive me. I fed on daily praise reports and testimonies and reading the Word, I sang much praise when I was desperate and the Lord calmed me. I changed to singing love songs that brought me into a deep intimacy with my HH. I read your books *How God Can and Will Restore Your Marriage* and *A Wise Woman*, each taught me how God wanted to change me to be a woman under His control according to the will of God.

What were the most difficult times that God helped you through, Alice?

The worst times were when I learned of other women and then again when I accepted God's will when I found out he was involved with OW. When he would spend time with her and he didn't want to come back to me, but just wanted to be with me from time to time.

It was very difficult to obey this principle of accepting it, of letting go, because even my best friend who accompanied me throughout this journey of separation was against this principle and prayed against me. But the Lord gave me a picture, it was amazing how the answers came.

Erin's Be Encouraged videos helped me a lot by answering my questions at the right time. And a lot of prayers helped me to stay focused on the journey I was on with Him.

Alice, what was the "turning point" of your restoration?

When I reached my limit, when I finally broke, and I spoke to the Lord telling Him that I couldn't take it anymore and was willing to let my husband go. I didn't want to be with him anymore or see him anymore.

It's when I became cold with him, disinterested that things turned around. I pretended to let go prior to this many times but he always saw through me. I know if I'd had the Lord where He should have been in my life and heart, letting go would have been much easier. But God allowed me to get to this place of brokenness, then I let go, and right away things changed. The worst part is that I left RMI thinking I should go because I didn't want restoration. But this is what they try to explain from the beginning but I didn't get it. Being here is to remain a wise woman, to become closer as His bride.

Tell us HOW it happened, Alice? Did your husband just walk in the front door? Alice, did you suspect or could you tell you were close to being restored?

When he realized my lack of interest was real, he was afraid of losing me and asked me, then begged me to return home.

Would you recommend any of our resources in particular that helped you, Alice?

I recommend all the resources from RMI, especially reading the daily praise reports and doing each of the recommended courses. A huge thanks to this ministry, and especially to Erin, thank you so much for surrendering yourself into God's hands so that He could use you in this wonderful way. How can I begin to tell you how much you've meant to me and to all of us?

I have been asking God to direct me so that I can be an instrument in His hands and help other women as you have, but as I said when I began my testimony I haven't done anything. I think it's because I have a hard time writing and expressing myself I feel inadequate.

Would you be interested in helping encourage other women, Alice?

Yes, I really want to help, but I didn't know how. I had been asking God for direction and am so thankful I came back when I did to find How to become a minister.

Either way, Alice, what kind of encouragement would you like to leave women with, in conclusion?

Do not give up on doing God's will. Give it all into His hands, do it without worry or despair, rest in Him and He will take care of the whole situation.

Chapter 27

Asia

"Be kind to one another, tender-hearted,
forgiving each other, just as God in Christ
also has forgiven you."
—Ephesians 4:32

"He Handed Me His Wedding Ring and Asked Me to Marry Him!"

Asia, how did your restoration actually begin?

After my son was born, our marriage turned cold. Being a mother was a big dream of mine so I started to live for my son and he became my first priority. As time went on, a child came with a new set of commitments, like not working as much, which meant my husband had to work more. It also came with a new set of appointments that didn't include my husband. Very soon we were both complaining about each of us having of lack of attention, a lack of affection and a lack of companionship towards the other.

Everything came crashing down the day I saw a series of messages from the OW "other woman" on my husband's cell phone and got so angry, it was the last straw for me. I kicked him out of our house on his birthday when I saw her message.

How did God change your situation, Asia, as you sought Him wholeheartedly?

A week after I made the decision to kick him out, I began to feel empty. I was sure I had made the right decision and should be relieved, but it wasn't what I was feeling. I started searching the internet on how to overcome a breakup and eventually shifted the focus to marriage restoration. Through another restoration site, I found the RMI link and downloaded the RYM book. It was a punch in the gut reading about me. It seemed like I was reading my own story. I found I was that person, I was quarrelsome, I was selfish, and I was a self-righteous woman just as Erin confessed to be.

When I found out how unpleasant I had been to live with, what my husband endured for many years of our marriage, I felt so ashamed and began to understand the reasons that made him walk away from me. First, I asked God for forgiveness for not being the wife He wished I had been, a wise woman who builds her house, who is meant to be the crown of her husband. After feeling so much lighter after this confession to Him, I began to feel forgiven and loved by Him. Next I asked my husband for forgiveness, now conscious of the behavior I should have exhibited as a gentle and quiet spirit. I continued to change the way I acted with my EH and with other people as well after each lesson in your free courses.

What principles, from God's Word (or through our resources), Asia, did the Lord teach you during this trial?

The first principle I put into practice was forgiveness, then letting go, which for me was a daunting task because I was always anxious and controlling. Then suddenly having to leave it all to Him and trust Him to do it, really required great effort on my part. I also incorporated submission whenever I had the opportunity, even though I was separated from my husband. Soon I was able to make the Lord my HH.

What were the most difficult times that God helped you through, Asia?

The time I suffered the most was during the Christmas holidays, when my husband took my son to travel with him leaving me alone. The second had to be when I learned so many unpleasant things from people close to my husband who told me what he was doing. At these times, I clung to the Lord even more, opened my heart to Him and His healing, and felt understood and loved by Him.

Asia, what was the "turning point" of your restoration?

It took me awhile to finally surrender my EH to the Lord and trust God to restore our marriage, but when that happened, I felt such a peace, a certainty that He would do His best for me, no matter what, because He was enough for me. I was finally happy, complete and fulfilled, and for me, all that mattered was Him.

I heard from my husband that this was when he noticed how quiet I was and that started to mess with him, causing him to want me back.

Tell us HOW it happened, Asia? Did your husband just walk in the front door? Asia, did you suspect or could you tell you were close to being restored?

When I realized that being nasty had hurt my husband so much, I became nice to him, respecting him. Little by little he got closer, invited me out, sometimes just with him, sometimes with our son.

When we sat down to talk he would say he was very hurt by what I'd done to him, but keeping quiet and listening and nodding my head, he went onto say how he could hardly believe how much I had changed.

We were intimate a few times, but the very next day, he always pretended that nothing had happened. Thankfully I'd read enough testimonies to know this was common and that the remedy was to just be excited that I had my HH and didn't need my EH. That was a huge shift and what helped gain momentum for restoration.

One day I came home from work and saw that someone had broken into my house. So my EH decided to stay over with me and my son because there was no way to secure the door. The next day he stayed over again and then decided to stay just a few days more. Each week he began staying a few days a week with us. At that point I started talking to God, asking if the end was near and I could feel the answer was yes.

The next week a cousin of mine was getting married and I asked my HH if I should invite my EH. So I invited him to come along and he accepted. When the wedding was over he took me to the altar, knelt down, took his wedding ring from his pocket, handed it to me and asked if I would forgive him and marry him again! I was shocked by how romantic it all was. I'd told my HH I didn't need anything like what I told him early on in my restoration journey, but just by letting that go of that too, He did something far better than I could ever have imagined. Asking forgiveness is nothing I needed, but He made it happen.

Would you recommend any of our resources in particular that helped you, Asia?

I recommend the book *How God Can and Will Restore Your Marriage* to give hope and awareness of what you are living. I also recommend *A Wise Woman* to teach you how to behave as you get closer to restoration and especially afterward. I'm so thankful for your free courses and all the encouragement I am able to find everywhere on your sites.

Would you be interested in helping encourage other women, Asia?

Yes

Either way, Asia, what kind of encouragement would you like to leave women with, in conclusion?

Dear brides, my separation lasted a year and 4 months. That sounds like a lot to outsiders, but to me it was the perfect amount of time, because it was God's appointed time for me to be renewed, to be healed and especially to know my Lord as the dearest Husband ever imagined. I enjoyed every minute I was alone with my Heavenly Husband, and I confess I have even missed the time I got to be alone with Him now that I'm restored. So enjoy your journey!

God knows why you haven't been restored yet, He knows all the reasons, and there is no doubt He is preparing you for something much better than you can imagine just as He did for me. I would never dream of my own husband asking for forgiveness at the altar and knowing this was His gift to me! He is faithful girls, do not lose faith.

Chapter 28

Kinsey

"...I and my maidens also will fast in the same way.
And thus I will go in to the king,
which is not according to the law;
and if I perish, I perish."
—Esther 4:16

"This Time It Would be Different"

Kinsey, how did your restoration actually begin?

It is with tears in my eyes that I write this because when I was praying for my marriage to be restored, I would look at this form and wonder when I would fill it out and share my testimony with the world. I thought it would take a lot of time or it might never happen. Now that the time is here, I'm really doing it, my heart is so full as I sit here ready to give God the praise He deserves!

It all started when my husband left home for the 6th or 7th time. There were so many times that he left me, I lost count. In the early days, I even found relief when he'd leave because I was suffering a lot with him when he was home. But the last time he left, that night I inexplicably began to feel something different about me, I understood that God wanted me to fight for my marriage once again, but this time He was saying it would be different.

So I asked the Lord, still very lost in my feelings, for Him to direct me to something that would help me get through this painful situation once and for all. It was then that the Holy Spirit touched me and led me to look for an old testimony of a missionary that someone had sent me months ago. The testimony was on Facebook, and I was amazed because it was just that morning I reactivated my Facebook after I had disabled it for a few weeks. I was afraid to see things on my husband's profile that would hurt me (because I knew something was going on I didn't want to face). I finally found the testimony and in the middle of it, there was a link to a book called *How God Can and Will Restore Your Marriage*. I was impressed with the statement of the title and decided to continue following His leading me, believing it was the direction I had asked the Lord for.

I started reading the book and realizing how wrong I was in my marriage, which was a shock because I thought that only he was wrong. I practically read the whole book in two days, writing down the verses and phrases that had the most to do with what I was going through. I felt an almost unbearable lump in my chest and throat. I cried all night, and I began to miss him for the first time ever.

At the same time, I remembered bad things he was doing to me and still felt like the poor victim. The first week I was also led to read the Bible sometimes until two in the morning plus reading from Erin's book and her website where I enrolled in Course 1. Erin's Be Encouraged eVideos were also answers to my questions and whenever I was going through something where I didn't know how to act, I watched the videos and there were all the answers I needed. God was in this, directing me, using Erin and this ministry as I traveled along this journey.

How did God change your situation, Kinsey, as you sought Him wholeheartedly?

God was molding me according to His will and each situation I encountered served to change me day by day. I could already feel peace even with him gone and without any news of what he was doing or where he was. When I was distressed, I read the testimonies of other women who'd come through this or worse. Many touched me a lot and taught me how to have faith and just let him go.

Letting go was very difficult. No longer talking to friends about my situation was also very difficult, but ultimately it was a release and immense freedom. I prayed and read the Word every day, several times a day. God was beginning to show me where I needed to change. Then it was time to realize how that change would happen. Excitedly I approached my Heavenly Husband, this time with all my heart. Yes, He became everything and every One to me. This was the part of my journey when He was with me every day and throughout the night. When I truly became His bride is when everything changed.

What principles, from God's Word (or through our resources), Kinsey, did the Lord teach you during this trial?

I learned many principles that I believe were crucial to my personal restoration and also for my marriage. One of them was winning without a word. I realized that our many discussions I forced on my husband did not change anything but actually made everything worse in our relationship. Another was letting him go. I disappeared from his sight, I didn't answer any of the messages that he had sent me during the first few weeks.

Unfortunately I had a relapse and went back to his Facebook and saw that he had changed the status of married to single and removed all the photos of us together. I thought he was already living his single life while I was crying for our marriage, which was the final blow that convinced me I needed a Heavenly Husband who I knew adored me and would "never leave or forsake me." Once again I deleted Facebook and went back to dedicating myself only to seek God and do His will — making my HH first in my life and heart.

What were the most difficult times that God helped you through, Kinsey?

The second week into my journey is when I found out that he had erased our memories from the social network and thought himself "no longer married." It was the hardest time, but through the Courses, the testimonies, the reading of Psalms and Proverbs, and both the devotionals, I came through it. I didn't have my HH then, not yet, so it was one of the most difficult things I needed to come through while staying on the right course. Erin taught me that I was rescuing myself, by no longer fighting in the flesh, instead, standing by while God fought for me.

Of course, several weeks later, I had another relapse (after my Facebook mess) because I was very afraid of him being with someone else. I didn't reactivate my Facebook, but I looked when someone showed me from their phone that he had added two strange women from his past. My world collapsed and I battled a thousand new things that went round and round in my head. It was the worst thing, so stupid I fell for it. After the battle was won, by turning to Him in a new and greater way (I was on the 2nd Abundant Life course by this time), I recovered and went back to doing everything that Erin taught and did not let the doubt overtake me. Believing that I'd messed up too much or that I should try something different than the course He'd set for me, I believed the truth that He brought me here for a reason.

That day, I watched a video and read something that comforted me, where Erin said that when everything seemed to get worse, it was because the restoration was near and the enemy wanted to take my focus off the path.

Kinsey, what was the "turning point" of your restoration?

At this point in my journey, I read in the book that I needed to find two people to fast with me because the three-fold cord does not break. That day I received another message from him saying if he could come to our house on Saturday to get his documents. I said yes, and I contacted two people I trust to fast for three days with me. We fasted and waited for Saturday to ask God to direct me in everything, what to say, how to dress, to listen more than speak and do everything that God instructed me to do.

Tell us HOW it happened, Kinsey? Did your husband just walk in the front door? Kinsey, did you suspect or could you tell you were close to being restored?

Although he had arranged to pick up the documents to file for divorce, I was very afraid of ruining everything, but God had already done the hard work in me, completely changing me. That contentious woman had died, and I was ready to forgive and ask for forgiveness, even if he insisted on divorce. I was ready for anything because my trust in my Heavenly Husband was greater than anything—I knew that He would do the best. I had determined this would be a new harder phase of my journey. I never thought for a moment that this would be the day, my restoration would happen.

So on Saturday, I prepared my house, bathed as Queen Esther had to prepare herself for her task. I asked if he came, if he did show up, my husband would walk in and feel overwhelming peace. I finished getting ready and perfumed myself because my HH told me that we were going to have a wonderful night of love. Even though I thought it was crazy, I obeyed my Lord. He also directed me to go to the bakery and buy his favorite snack because he would be hungry and would lunch with me that day. Again, as crazy as it felt, I did so, fully trusting what my HH was saying to me. I turned on my Love Song and began to fall in love with my Beloved like never before. I told my HH that I wanted Him. He was all I wanted, all I needed, all I lived for.

When he finally arrived, I asked him to please come in using a sweet voice. He said he was just there to get his documents. He was calm but I could see he was afraid. So I felt that I should ask him to sit down and talk. To my surprise, he accepted and listened to me. I said I didn't want a divorce and I apologized for some things I did that I remembered at the time, but that if divorce would make him happy, then I would be happy to sign. I told him he was free to go and how happy I was. He listened to me and after I finished, he said he forgave me. He said that during those weeks away from me, he had been thinking a lot and that he had seen how much he had been wrong what he'd done to me. He asked me to forgive him and the hate-wall fell.

As I continued to listen, winning without a word, he asked me if I would accept him back. I smiled and knew that I was witnessing the beginning of the restoration of our marriage. Feeling my HH again, I got up and walked over to sit next to him, and without saying a word, I stroked him on the cheek. He was reluctant at first, but then tears filled his eyes as he caressed my face and we hugged each other. It was all so beautiful and romantic, I could feel the presence of my Heavenly Love there with me. I was loving my earthly husband with the love of my Heavenly Husband.

We had our moment of love as if it were intimate for the first time. Afterward, we listened to the praise music (he'd ask me to turn it on) and peace washed over us. We said nothing, just felt each other's presence and His presence was there with us.

A few hours later, he said he was hungry and I laughed when I remembered what my HH had told me to do. I prepared his lunch and sat in silence as he ate. In my heart, I thanked my Heavenly Husband over and over that day because my earthly husband was there, with me. While laying on his side of the bed, he said that he loved me. It was the dream He'd promised. It was faster than I thought and what I had prepared myself for. All I can say is that everything Erin teaches in her free courses, in her books, and in her videos work. I obeyed and trusted God, not Erin because I knew that all the principles she lovingly taught were for me to learn. I came to my appointed time in my life and trusted God to restore my marriage.

My marriage was restored to the honor and glory of the name of the Lord! Thank you, Erin and all the women who make up her Ministry Team. I keep taking the courses and reading the materials because my husband is not saved yet, but I think he will soon be after completing the SS course. Each of the courses aren't just for restoration but helping us be better women and find true love at last. A love only our HH can give us!

Would you recommend any of our resources in particular that helped you, Kinsey?

I recommend the *How God Can and Will Restore Your Marriage* book and even if you've read the book, go through Course 1 to get started. To stay on course, reading Psalms and Proverbs and devotionals daily. Be Encouraged eVideos for comfort. Then, it's important to find your Heavenly Love by going through each of the Abundant Life Courses.

Would you be interested in helping encourage other women, Kinsey?

YES, God has already sent me one woman to encourage right now and I have already recommended the courses and books. I hope to do more in the future.

Either way, Kinsey, what kind of encouragement would you like to leave women with, in conclusion?

Give your life totally to God. Next, give your heart to your Heavenly Husband. Only He cares for you and will never forsake you. You need this kind of love to make the changes necessary. Get away from people who tell you to give up and take care of your life yourself. Don't investigate his life, let him go. Get off Facebook until you can use it for good to minister to women. Follow everything that is taught in the book. Do not listen to rumors or lies. Do not doubt why God brought you here. Remember, nothing is impossible for God.

Chapter 29

Malena

"Delight yourself in the Lord;
And He will give you the desires of your heart."
—Psalm 37:4

"The Dream I'd Thought was Dead—
He Made Alive!!"

Malena, how did your restoration actually begin?

Dear brides, it is with great joy that I am here to tell you that I have been restored since the beginning of the year. Forgive me for the delay in submitting my testimony because I know just how important it is for us to read the testimonies. The testimonies encouraged me to keep going, to set my focus on my HH and then I failed to submit my own! Due to the suddenness, the complete change in my life, lack of internet time with a husband home (as they warn us will happen) and the mistake I made when I stopped the courses (now I'm back with a new more intense focus on Him and am determined to stay here!!) is why I failed you all and did not send my testimony until now. But Praise God that our HH loves us so much that He forgives us when we simply ask and gives us chance after chance to get it right. Your mercies are new every morning and have no end. Hallelujah!!! :)

After being separated for more than eight years, in January my husband called me out of the blue saying he wanted to come back to us (me and our 4 children). I was living with my mother at the time and he was living with his mother (after many OWs came and went through his life). So we decided we should live together and stay with my mother-in-law to avoid paying rent after my husband said it was time to start building our dream house, a new home where we could have a new fresh start. We had already purchased the land and the dream I'd thought was dead and gone He made alive again!!

How did God change your situation, Malena, as you sought Him wholeheartedly?

After being with RMI for forever, I finally decided to stop holding onto my "dream" of a restored marriage. I never let go. I said I did, but I held onto my EH in my heart and God knew it. Then one day, I simply gave everything to my HH, I could no longer live without Him as so many testified to Him being in their lives. He became my First Love, my Everything, my Provider, my Comforter, my Savior who would save me from myself and my selfish desires. The Beloved of my soul. Whenever something happened to discourage or hurt me, I would give it all to Him. I would cry to Him and rest in His arms of love. When the pain was so strong that I could not even talk to Him or hear Him (because just as Erin says things are going to get heated when you get close) I sang love songs to Him and He enveloped me—oh, what a sweet Presence I bathed in!!! When He was all I could see, I no longer could see my afflictions but only saw by faith, through His eyes.

Certainly, I cared nothing for restoration anymore, truly knowing in my heart of hearts that it did not matter because I had who I wanted and who I lived for—that's when all things work together for good to those who love God. It's when everything in my life changed.

One thing I am sure I LOVE my HH for who He is, not for what He can give me, not anymore!!!!!!!

When I think of how long I held on, ignored the main principle of letting go, of thinking I could hold onto my dream, my promise of a restored marriage, while all along I was missing out on the real pearls (like that story that I read somewhere on a praise report or lesson).

What principles, from God's Word (or through our resources), Malena, did the Lord teach you during this trial?

I learned that I wasn't as submissive to my new Husband as I needed to be. Instead, I realized that I was in spiritual adultery, my restoration, my estranged husband, were both above my Heavenly Husband in my heart.

I learned that I must be a sweet, kind, virtuous woman and stop pretending to be. I told everyone (including myself) that I was doing everything, following all the principles, when deep down I was committing spiritual adultery. This ministry was God's vessel to sustain me on this journey and teach me to be His alone. They never give up on what is important. I know they get a lot of women who attack them on this, and no wonder. It's life-changing becoming His bride. Everyone wants their man back no matter what they have to do. But to do it HIS way, with HIS priorities is going to mean you're setting yourself up to be under enemy attack and lies to try and stop you.

What were the most difficult times that God helped you through, Malena?

There were so many over these past 8 years. Probably the most difficult was when I learned of 2 OWs who my husband got pregnant. Later I found out they were lying (though they could have been his). The other that I battled through was when my young teenage son was spending the weekend with his father and came back really quiet. After he agreed to let me pray for him, he told me he saw his dad kissing one of the OW. He was literally sick to his stomach. At the time, I thought I could never forgive what he'd done. After several months of being away from my HH, not feeling His presence (due to not forgiving) I realized there was no way out unless I forgave. That's when I found Erin's truth "who can forgive but God alone" when she explained how she forgave her husband. How we just need to be real with the Lord, tell Him how we feel, that we don't want to forgive, that he doesn't deserve to be forgiven... just tell Him everything and then say, "You need to do it, I surrender" and that's when immediately the burden was lifted. I also relapsed a few times and had to repeat this but each time I felt so clean, so at peace.

Malena, what was the "turning point" of your restoration?

At dawn, my husband texted me from his cell phone. At this point, he had stopped talking to me almost entirely. If he did text it was to spew out angry harsh words of contempt to hurt me (that was due to not letting go) and then he said he was desperate, asking me not to give up on him, that he loved me, to please never stop praying for him and begging me to wait for him. He texted a couple of hours later to please not to get someone else (I did not reply to his first text). That's when he told me he had just dreamed that I was radiant with happiness because I was in love with another man, a man who took good care of our children and was supplying all our needs. This new man in my life took such good care of me that he woke up sweating and shaking, desperate to find out and that's when he sent me a text message.

Our HH has a sense of humor, sending my husband a dream that caused him such a feeling of losing me, which is nonetheless absolutely true!

The entire turn of events happened once the Lord was my HH and first love! Once I was honest, that restoration no longer mattered. When I was honestly and truly happy with my life as it was, without my earthly husband is when God saw I was ready to have my marriage restored!! The moment I no longer wanted restoration, as soon as I began to focus my HH as the most important in my life. Yes, that was the turning point, when I no longer thought about anything or anyone and I just wanted my HH!!!!!

Tell us HOW it happened, Malena? Did your husband just walk in the front door? Malena, did you suspect or could you tell you were close to being restored?

Never in a million years did I think it was close. I think it was because I no longer cared or I would have seen the signs. Without noticing any of the signs, when he texted then came over, standing there in front of me after not seeing him in years!!! When I didn't even want restoration, I loved living alone with my HH. I wanted time alone with Him, to sing love songs to Him, to meditate on the Word, realizing each was His promise to me, love letters to me.

As of today, we've now been together for almost a full year. Next month we will celebrate our anniversary for the first time in 9 years. I am a new woman and he is a new man, husband, father, son, brother. Imagine, a new man and I know the best is yet to come. I can only say THANK YOU, THANK YOU, THANK YOU to my HH, to Erin, to the ministers and to each of you who continued to share your praise and love for Him!!!! He used you all to give me a new life!

Would you recommend any of our resources in particular that helped you, Malena?

Yes. Start your day with daily encouragement, take one of the courses, read Psalms and Proverbs. Most important has to be knowing how to live your abundant life with your HH.

Would you be interested in helping encourage other women, Malena?

Yessssss! Yes I would!

Either way, Malena, what kind of encouragement would you like to leave women with, in conclusion?

Look at Him only. Have your HH as your main and only focus. Let go of your restoration, your EH and everything else you're hanging onto. Your life is His. What looks like an endless desert will suddenly change to streams in the desert once you stop ignoring what you know you must do. Let this ministry teach you to depend on Him and to live His perfect and pleasant will for you, your family life and your marriage. Trust Him and follow EVERYTHING in this ministry as it is 100% Word-based. Listen to no lies, rumors or anything else that is meant to steal what He has for you!

Chapter 30

Antoinette

"When you were dead in your transgressions
and the uncircumcision of your flesh,
He made you alive together with Him,
having forgiven us all our transgressions."
—Colossians 2:13

"Emotionally and Spiritually Dead— Alive Again—Guilt and Fear Gone!"

Antoinette, how did your restoration actually begin?

It all started with my husband telling me that he would leave home. It was the second time he left. At first, I was really happy, the idea of him being gone because for more than three years we'd been in crisis mode. Neither one of us was happy being married. We'd been together for 15 years, 9 years being married, 3 children and countless mistakes made by both of us.

The end of the road for him happened after I had confessed to having kissed a coworker during an office party. We were both drunk, but that didn't matter. He always had a hard time forgiving, and that was the beginning of the end for us. After staying together for two years, trying to forgive me, my husband finally said outright that he could not forgive me. That stupid mistake wiped out every good feeling that ever existed for him.

So since I was tired because I had already paid dearly for my mistake, I thought, "Good, if that was what he wants, great, goodbye." I just wanted to put an end to this story that had already gone on for far too long. So he left.

About 3 weeks later the night after I'd been at a birthday party with my children, I woke up and I felt that God did not want the end of my marriage. So the next day I called my attorney, dropped the divorce and started searching the internet for something to guide me. Somehow (that I know was God) I found a post on Instagram and it offered a PDF for the first chapter of the book *How God Can and Will Restore Your Marriage*. I read the first chapter, I reread it three times, then went to your Hope At Last website that was also posted. I filled out the evaluation and started the courses. I bought *A Wise Woman*, and took every single course available.

How did God change your situation, Antoinette, as you sought Him wholeheartedly?

God took all the blindness from my eyes. I was already spiritually dead. I grew up in the church but without any real relationship with the Lord. With no feelings left for anything or anyone, doing the simplest things was almost impossible. I didn't eat, I didn't talk to anyone, I didn't leave the house. My family and friends were worried thinking that I had depression, but just reading the RYM that I also ordered, along with looking up all the verses from the Word from God, I make the 3x5 cards that I kept with me. As I meditated on the Word, with a focus on Psalms and Proverbs every day, along with praising Him no matter how bad the circumstances, I was able to take every depressed or fearful thought captive. Because I couldn't eat, I used not eating, as fasting—soon enough He healed me! I began to eat, I began to feel again, I was thankful and pleased to be alive, to enjoy the simple things in life. I was emotionally and spiritually dead—then I was finally alive again—all guilt and fear were gone!

What principles, from God's Word (or through our resources), Antoinette, did the Lord teach you during this trial?

Prayer, total obedience to the Word that I found in your books. Letting go of anger, unforgiveness, shame and every other negative feeling that wanted to drown me in depression. I also stopped speaking about my situation to anyone, thinking somehow this would make me feel better (to get people to understand how I was feeling) when in fact it kept me depressed and chained to my past. Continually checking to see if there was any sin in me, like not forgiving. Agreeing with my husband (when he'd fling insults at me) and just praying for the Lord to deliver me. I also began to sow hope in others with every social media I had, offering links and RYM Chapter 1. I also discovered that after I tithe to my storehouse, RMI and let go of attending church, I was able to cling to the Lord and He became my Heavenly Husband.

What were the most difficult times that God helped you through, Antoinette?

Probably the biggest test came the day he came over to pick up the children for a visit. When I got in the car to put my son in the car seat, I saw a woman's jacket laying on the front seat. If I had not been firmly grounded in His principles, promises, and fasting at the time, I would never have been able to obey the Lord who was telling me not to react. Instead, I would have made a huge scene and broken everything in sight, I would have strangled him with the jacket and made him disappear from my life! But I did nothing, I just folded the jacket nicely and placed it back on the front seat. It was very difficult at first to live this way, but I was learning to depend totally on the Lord and He always surprised me by showing me the new woman I was becoming.

Antoinette, what was the "turning point" of your restoration?

One Sunday, my husband came to visit the children and told me that the next day, on Monday, that he was going to file for divorce. I smiled because I was looking to the LORD, so my face was beautifully radiant when my husband started praising me! I followed the Lord as He led me to buy a snack for him for his drive home, a snack I'd forgotten he liked. As he was about to leave, I handed it to him and my husband said (later) he suddenly noticed there was something different about me. As he stared, he asked if he could give me a friendly hug, making it clear that our marriage was over but he wanted us to remain friends. I agreed, hugged him back, smiled and waved as he drove away.

Tell us HOW it happened, Antoinette? Did your husband just walk in the front door? Antoinette, did you suspect or could you tell you were close to being restored?

On Monday (I found out later), he didn't go to the lawyers. The next week, on my birthday, he asked me if it was alright if he came home. After I completed that 3rd abundant life book and started practicing biblical principles in it, is when my marriage was restored.

Would you recommend any of our resources in particular that helped you, Antoinette?

I recommend all the ministry resources, books *How God Can and Will Restore Your Marriage* also *A Wise Woman*, *Testimony books* to study. Reading the Daily Encouragement, taking all your Courses, keeping up with the daily devotionals, Tithing to your storehouse. Each and everything is based on God's Word.

Would you be interested in helping encourage other women, Antoinette?

Yes!!!!

Either way, Antoinette, what kind of encouragement would you like to leave women with, in conclusion?

Nothing is too hard for the Lord. I started this journey thinking it was impossible, but I knew and saw with my own eyes the God of the impossible. Before I only heard, but then I saw. He inclines any heart even the hardest of stone towards Him. Please, don't give up, obey without fear, and seek Him until He becomes your Great Love.

Chapter 31

Maeve

"The woman said to Him,
'Sir, give me this water, so I will not be thirsty
nor come all the way here to draw.'"
—John 4:15

"I Was the Woman at the Well"

Maeve, how did your restoration actually begin?

Before I start my testimony I'd like to share a little bit more about my journey. First I want to praise my Beloved HH who is the best Lover and who has healed me of every fear. Because He was so patient and loving with me at all times I am not the frightened broken woman who began this journey.

I always read the testimonies and believed that one day I would read mine. To think that this day has actually arrived is such a miracle!!

In my relationship I was the opposite of the woman He created me to be. I was just like everyone who He calls to come here. I was contentious, manipulative, fragile, spiteful, hypocritical and unfaithful at various times in our life together... I was rotten to the core!!

In the last months before we broke up we were fighting a lot! And the reasons were always so silly in comparison to other crises that we had previously. I always told him that someday we would separate and then it really happened. The mouth spoke what the heart was full of. The push to separate as always was mine and when I tried to go back, my partner did not want me anymore. I loved to manipulate him, to pretend that I wanted to separate just to see him crawling and begging at my feet. He always struggled to keep our family together, as I was constantly pulling it down, but this time he got tired and that's when I woke up in utter despair.

I spent the following weeks begging him to reconcile, just once more. He agreed to stay, but only for a few days, but that's when he asked to be transferred so that he could work in another state. So we didn't see each other for more than 6 months. God really got my attention removing "lover and friend far from me." I was truly a "loathing" to him.

So I stayed behind living with my 2 daughters from a previous relationship in a state where I didn't know anyone. Yes, it was painful because we were the sort of couple who always did everything together. Being so ashamed at what I'd done, I just shared my situation with my sister, to help me in prayer, but kept everything else to myself.

How did God change your situation, Maeve, as you sought Him wholeheartedly?

I felt insecure wondering if God was going to restore my relationship because I was not legally married, although there was a hint of hope in my heart. I looked for various testimonies of a restored relationship from someone who wasn't married but found nothing. I confess that I was frustrated. Whenever I was working during the day my situation flashed through my mind but when I got home, I was consumed with fear and all I could do was cry.

During the first 2 months I suffered a lot. I was not in the mood for trying anything and thought a lot of nonsense, worthless ways to fix my life and relationship. Then one day on Facebook I saw someone posting something about RMI, I just knew it was the Lord who directed me to your site. I immediately devoured the website, submitted the questionnaire and downloaded the book, *How God Can and Will Restore Your Marriage* on my cell phone, because I had no money to buy the book. Reading just the first chapter I saw that my situation was not lost, not in the least hopeless. Oh my heart was filled with joy because I felt God was talking to me.

There was a day that I came home from work and after crying a lot I asked my HH to fill the void in my heart, saying I didn't want to cry for my ex-partner anymore. From that day on I started to feel a sense of peace and I only remembered him at night but instead of crying I felt joy because I had the best Husband.

I started taking courses and feeding on His Word. I was overjoyed when I read "Married to my Son's Father" confirming that God did have a plan for women like me. I was the woman at the well, not married to the man I had been living with, John 4:4-42.

I stuck the verses I wanted to sow into my heart and on my closet door to read every night and every morning:

"Delight yourself in the Lord and He will grant your heart's desires." Psalm 37:4.

"Seek first the kingdom of God and His justice and all things will be added to you." Matthew 6:33.

On my journey I fell and got up several times, but it was the unconditional love of my HH who never gave up on me that kept me moving forward.

What principles, from God's Word (or through our resources), Maeve, did the Lord teach you during this trial?

I started to apply the teachings of letting go (it was not easy), winning without words, having a meek and quiet spirit and also fasting (which I thought was impossible for me).

I had just reconciled with the Lord after 10 years of being away, so I read His Word, prayed and sought His presence more than anything.

What were the most difficult times that God helped you through, Maeve?

The most difficult times were when I noticed him emotionally moving away from me more and more. We went months without speaking until one Saturday afternoon he called me.

Maeve, what was the "turning point" of your restoration?

When I handed my relationship over to God and asked Him to do His will and not mine. Then the second part was being my HH's Bride.

Tell us HOW it happened, Maeve? Did your husband just walk in the front door? Maeve, did you suspect or could you tell you were close to being restored?

After 4 months he suddenly appeared out of nowhere. He was on my doorstep at 1 in the morning. He spent a few days with us and then returned again to his mother's home and later to the new city he'd been transferred to (later I found out he asked for the transfer to move back near me).

The days he stayed at our home, we slept together but there was no intimacy. I kept reminding myself not to displease my HH and when he'd attempted anything, I lovingly refused but didn't explain why.

At the end of that month he said he would come home because he was now unemployed. I knew God was getting his attention. After being home for almost 3 weeks still living as friends, God turned his heart and completed the work He'd started. A new dream of mine was to be married. I never wanted to marry, most of my friends still don't think being married is the way to go, so I never married and neither had my partner. But then I learned how this was God's plan.

The week he arrived he asked if I wanted to go with him to church and he reconciled with the Lord and even went down to the altar. That's when the pastor asked about his relationship with me and offered to marry us. We married in a simple ceremony and can't believe I'm a married woman.

Even though I am married and no longer living sinfully I am still in the process of much refinement, believing and trusting the Lord with my life and that of my family. I trust that He will continue the necessary changes in all of us. I always told the Lord that I wanted to shout to the world "as for me and my house, we will serve the Lord." Joshua 24:15 and now I'm doing that too!!!

Would you recommend any of our resources in particular that helped you, Maeve?

I recommend that everyone use all the resources you offer. I used the books *How God Can and Will Restore Your Marriage* and *A Wise Woman*. I took most of your courses and am still taking them. My husband said he wanted to study *A Wise Man*.

Ministry Note: Each woman (or man) who submits a restored marriage testimony is sent a free couple's packet that includes both A Wise Woman and A Wise Man paperback books.

Would you be interested in helping encourage other women, Maeve?

Yes

Either way, Maeve, what kind of encouragement would you like to leave women with, in conclusion?

Beloved bride, I want to tell you never to give up, however painful it may be, trust Him who can do all things. He is the God of the impossible and loves to give us our heart's desire when He is all we want and all we need.

When you think you don't have the strength to continue, ask Him to renew your strength and give you the wisdom needed to overcome difficulties.

"The king's heart is like a brook of flowing water in the hands of the LORD." Proverbs 21:1.

"Praise the name of God forever and ever; wisdom and power belong to him. It changes times and seasons; dethrone kings and establish them. Give wisdom to the wise and knowledge to those who know how to discern." Daniel 2:20-21.

Chapter 32

Nia

"Be devoted to one another in brotherly love;
give preference to one another in honor;
not lagging behind in diligence, fervent in spirit,
serving the Lord; rejoicing in hope,
persevering in tribulation, devoted to prayer..."
—Romans 12:10-12

"Pain and Rejection Almost became Unbearable"

Nia, how did your restoration actually begin?

There is so much joy in my heart right now! God kept His promise and changed my life.

I was separated for just a little over a year soon after I discovered my husband had cheated on me and my husband left the next month when I told him he had to choose me or her. There was so much pain and suffering in those early days. I did not forgive him for what he did and the hurt only increased because I chose not to forgive him.

A month later, praise God, I was invited to join a group of women who were studying *A Wise Woman*. What a unique and life-changing moment in my life! Reading a WW made me see the value of the family and reflect on my role as wife, who during the nine years of my house I was completely foolish and gave the enemy several loopholes to steal and destroy my family. I tore my own house down besides never building it on the Rock. I had no idea what God said about anything but I began to learn.

When I finally told the women in the group that my husband had left, one woman smiled and said she was married to a Prodigal too and told me about the standers ministry she was part of. I began reading how to get my husband back but that's when so many horrible things began to happen. After that, many bad situations and one of the worst was when my husband told me that the "church" hurt me because I was having a false hope that nothing would make him come home, to me or to our daughters. He told me to leave him alone and told me he was thinking of remarrying the OW that I later read in a lesson is what happens when you don't let go.

How did God change your situation, Nia, as you sought Him wholeheartedly?

God always tried to talk to me through my sisters in the church and the several standers groups I attended, but as I listened to them and I believed that I could change him and make him want me again, the pain and rejection almost became unbearable.

At the end of the summer, when I was almost out of all hope and strength to fight for my marriage, I said a prayer on Sunday asking God for a sign whether or not I was going to continue this fight, why I couldn't continue to be so humiliated anymore. On Wednesday, at the women's service, a sister approached me and said she would email me a book she had received from a friend, and she believed that the book could give me strategies on how I could fight for the restoration of my family. OH GLORY!!!! At that moment a shock surged through me. I just knew it was God's answer to my prayer. She sent me Erin's book, *How God Can and Will Restore Your Marriage* and my God my life changed.

God spoke to me so much through that book. I discovered that I had lost my husband because I was so contentious, silly, quarrelsome, did not please Him, and mainly did not seek the Lord with all my heart. Then I pushed my husband away, made him hate me and despise me and be forced to treat me badly because I would not let go! From then on, I started looking for my HH only, I began being intimate with Him as my Husband and letting myself be transformed by His Love!

What principles, from God's Word (or through our resources), Nia, did the Lord teach you during this trial?

God showed me a lot through His Word. I searched for His Word every day, through the daily reading of the Bible. I bought the recommended Scourby app and read through the Bible for the first time in my life and challenged the women in my former standers group to do the same. I also bought a bunch of RYM books and left them with the paperback at the end of my last group meeting. I read the Psalms everyday and was running to Him at the moment I felt even the slightest pain or fear. When my HH was all I wanted and needed I was able to fully let my husband go (I stopped contacting him right away and got off all social media). My time was spent searching for more of the Lord, tirelessly reading everything on your website and reread the book, *How God Can and Will Restore Your Marriage*, dozens of times.

What were the most difficult times that God helped you through, Nia?

The Lord helped me to rid myself of all the anguish that was in my heart. He filled my heart with His peace so that I would not suffer from the circumstances and so I could learn to trust Him always.

Nia, what was the "turning point" of your restoration?

The turning point of our restoration was when I let go of every single situation and handed it over to God. I spoke to my HH and I surrendered everything to Him and let Him control everything in my life.

Tell us HOW it happened, Nia? Did your husband just walk in the front door? Nia, did you suspect or could you tell you were close to being restored?

A friend of his from the church (we had once attended as a couple) got to know my husband and decided to befriend him. One day he asked my husband if he wanted to attend a men's retreat and my husband accepted the invitation. The women were also having a retreat at the same time and I also decided to go. I had let go of attending church, but a friend asked me to come to support her because she was sharing her testimony. So I went for her, not for me.

At the luncheon I saw him and he saw me. I was shocked when my husband walked over, sat down, and began crying asking for my forgiveness. I said, "Of course, and hope you will forgive me."

During our conversation he said he would never leave us again, and from that day, our house would serve the Lord. He said he hoped to be the spiritual leader of our home and that our life and family would belong to the Lord. We left and drove home in his car. I had come with my friend :). That day we spent the rest of the time with our daughters as a real family!

Since coming home, God has been helping us to align everything according to His Word.

Would you recommend any of our resources in particular that helped you, Nia?

I recommend the book, *How God Can and Will Restore Your Marriage,* and the courses on your website. This daily spiritual feeding strengthens us a lot and gives us the wisdom to continue these spiritual struggles. I also purchased the WOTT packet so I could mark and study the testimonies to be able to overcome the wicked that was coming against my mind.

Would you be interested in helping encourage other women, Nia?

Yes, I am very interested in helping other women who are going through what I went through. I am already encouraging a close friend who I believe will soon receive her miracle and her family will be serving the Lord too.

Either way, Nia, what kind of encouragement would you like to leave women with, in conclusion?

Beloved brides, believe in the Word and His promises. Seek Him (not your husband) with all your heart, surrender your heartache, bad situations, even your lack of faith to Him and let Him fill you with peace and His Love. Believe His Word, because as Erin says, "you must believe that 'all things [can] work together for good to those who love God and are called according to His purpose'" Romans 8:28.

Continue your journey holding His hand, because God says, "But whoever endures to the end, he will be saved" Matthew 24:13. I challenge you to read through the Bible to be filled with hope through His Word. Reading the Bible will heal you, His promises will redeem your mind from lies. Be sure to "Rejoice in hope, be patient in the tribulation, persevere in prayer" Romans 12:12 and the more He will do on your behalf.

Your marriage will be restored because "Blessed is the man who suffers temptation; because when he is tried, he will receive the crown of life, which the Lord has promised to those who love Him" James 1:12. Let's all shout, "Amen!!"

Chapter 33

Ximena

"The mind of man plans his way,
But the Lord directs his steps."
—Proverbs 16:9

"No One Saw Me Cry"

Ximena, how did your restoration actually begin?

It all started when in a dream God warned me of the struggle that I would soon have and yet, I was disobedient and did not prepare for the battle to come. I continued living my life, inside the church (I am the leader of the women's group). I actually thought I had God in my life and that I knew Him and He knew me. But I was dead and cold, a whitewashed tomb, a Pharisee and I thought of myself as a super believer. How arrogant. What a big mistake and what sin, to be proud of what I thought I had.

Even so, God kept drawing me to Him, but I was blind and I didn't realize that like a fool I destroyed my house and tore it down. But He had mercy on me. A friend asked me for help regarding her broken marriage and I invited her to attend the ladies' worship when I heard that there would be a speaker who could help her. The funny thing is that she couldn't even go, but I went and the speaker shared her testimony. She said GOD had restored her marriage. God was already talking to me and preparing me for what would happen later that day. The same day God revealed to me that my husband was with an OW. Though I hadn't meant to, God made sure I heard enough to know what was happening. Thank God I didn't despair or panic because I already knew it was a spiritual war, and the first step was to unleash His forgiveness.

I thought everything would return to normal, but even though I forgave him, he kept fighting against staying at home and I was left struggling in prayer and fasting and seeking the face of God so that the crisis and desert land would end. During this time I faced many struggles and an amazing journey of discovering the ways of God. Then I came across several restoration sites, and the testimonies were fundamental to not give up, and then I discovered RMI and I put into practice the principles of the book *How God Can and Will Restore Your Marriage*.

I was often sad when I read the testimonies and saw that all the spouses left and sometimes even divorced their wives and then returned home. Since mine never left and I didn't know how a restoration could happen if the spouse didn't leave, but our GOD is the GOD of the impossible and He works differently in each of our lives! In total, my husband only spent 3 days away from home, but he never managed to get his things and leave us for good.

How did God change your situation, Ximena, as you sought Him wholeheartedly?

God continued to draw me to Him, and the more I was reading and rereading the book *How God Can and Will Restore Your Marriage* and I put into practice the principle of letting go (even though he was at my side inside the house), it was very painful and difficult. But you encouraged me to look to GOD, I did and He HELPED me. I went to Him in every crisis, made Him my Heavenly Husband, asked for forgiveness for anything and everything He revealed I'd done wrong. I asked Him to forgive me for being foolish, for being a Pharisee, for thinking I knew Him when I never did. I asked Him to forgive me for not having adored Him with all my heart, for not fasting, for not looking for Him in the early hours when He wanted to meet with me.

It's when I put all this into practice that everything in my life began to be reshaped and modified. It's then that GOD transformed me, and the best, most wonderful thing began to happen. I began to see changes that HE was doing in my husband's life. I still long for him to give GOD his life because he has not yet come to Him fully. But I am grateful for everything as I still trust to see the salvation of my husband and his family.

What principles, from God's Word (or through our resources), Ximena, did the Lord teach you during this trial?

The LORD taught me a lot during my journey, He taught me to pray, to trust Him, to not to look at the circumstances. I learned that HE is my Husband, and that I was never a true Believer and I didn't even know it. He taught me to meditate on the Word and reading through the

Bible in order to discover this and so much more. I learned to fast, not to give all our love and attention to our earthly husbands, and to put our HH first place in our lives.

What were the most difficult times that God helped you through, Ximena?

When he disappeared for 3 days, I wanted to call, to go looking for him. I was also afraid that our family and neighbors would find out. I was so thankful when I read the book and I discovered that I didn't need to share what was going on with others. My family didn't need to know (and still doesn't know what I went through), because He was all I needed. The enemy kept trying to humiliate me, but he didn't manage to uncover what was happening. Through it all, I fought the enemy by remaining His servant, smiled as I walked in our neighborhood or met anyone on the street. I smiled when I went to church (before He became my Spiritual Leader and I let go of attending). These darkest days are when I was the happiest of all. No one saw me cry or walk with my head down. If I cried, I cried to GOD and He consoled me with His Word and reminded me of His promises.

Even when he told me his decision was to stay with the OW and gave me details of how he was welcomed into her in her family, I just stood by while I watched the Lord fight for me and He won because He doesn't lose battles. He always succeeds. As no one supported him, he decided to leave everyone and me and my daughter, but who is the head of man? It's the Lord and GOD the head of everyone. The enemy failed. My husband tried to put his plans into action, but GOD foiled his attempt. When he took her to meet his family, God supported me, He gave me favor. I thought it was the end, but I focused on how much I adored Him and sought Him with my whole heart. I didn't focus on restoration and this transformed me into a new creature. They never managed to enter the house, my mother-in-law stopped them before they were able to go inside. They were asked to leave and had to leave.

Tell us HOW it happened, Ximena? Did your husband just walk in the front door? Ximena, did you suspect or could you tell you were close to being restored?

Because he never really left, I believe my restoration happened when he decided not to leave. After he was convinced that he wanted the OW, after he said he wanted to be happy with her, that they planned to live in a new house, but GOD, turned his heart. God wouldn't let him go out or take his things from the house. And that night he left and spent 3 days away from home, he came back and finally told me he was done with her. God told him it was wrong.

GOD always consoled me with His Word. In Psalm 27:14 says, "wait on the Lord, cheer up, and He will strengthen your heart; wait on the Lord." That's what I did and as the days passed and he's heart continued to turn back to me. I saw how he was already being molded by GOD, he became affectionate again, saying that he and I were meant to be. He told me he realized how blind he was about her and how wrong he was to put us all through this. Every day I see how my husband is discovering something new about God as He is revealing Himself to him, and revealing his sins that he continues to confess to me.

Would you recommend any of our resources in particular that helped you, Ximena?

THE BOOK AS GOD CAN AND WILL RESTORE YOUR MARRIAGE, NOT ONLY READING ONCE BUT READING IT OVER AND OVER. EVERY TIME YOU FINISH YOU MUST START IT AGAIN. SO THAT ENEMY WILL NOT STEAL THE WORD FROM YOUR HEART, AND THE REPORTS AND TESTIMONIALS.

Would you be interested in helping encourage other women, Ximena?

Yes

Either way, Ximena, what kind of encouragement would you like to leave women with, in conclusion?

Never give up, nor look at the circumstances, because GOD does not work by sight, but through works by faith, 2 Corinthians 5:7 GOD does not see how man sees, 1 Samuel 16:7. The enemy plants lies and sets up circumstances to make you and me give up! He lies sending people to tell us things that are not true. He even uses our own husbands to hurt us, but if our faith is in GOD, He promises to turn the heart of man. Trust only GOD. THAT IS WHO SUPPORTS US, AND DESERVES OUR LOVE!

Chapter 34

Camille

"Ask, and it will be given to you; seek, and you will find;
knock, and it will be opened to you.
For everyone who asks receives,
and he who seeks finds,
and to him who knocks it will be opened."
—Matthew 7:7-8

"God Who Brought My EH Home — Not Me!"

Camille, how did your restoration actually begin?

It began when my husband came home on a Monday after work and told me that we needed to talk. He said that he was not happy and that he thought it was better for us to be separated. While he was telling me that, he was crying, which surprised me because in the nine years we have been together I have seen him cry only twice. I didn't know what to say to him, because he had already left me more than once before, so I knew this time was different.

The first time my husband left after I'd told him that I no longer knew if I loved him. He was hurt by what I said, so he packed a bag and left. The next time he left I'd told him to get out during a fight but of course, it wasn't long before I regretted it and asked him to come back. He was gone a total of three weeks before he came back home.

The third time this happened, the final time, was when we were having another argument when I told him to "just leave." This time when I asked him to come back, he came back right away but I noticed he was really distant and cold with me. So I asked him what was going on because he was already showing signs of something that was very wrong. He didn't say anything, so I demanded to know why he didn't turn his cell phone on at home anymore, he didn't let me get his cell phone, and also why he changed his password on his phone. Then I told him I noticed I no longer had access to his social network, that the password had been changed. And that's when he told me that he wanted to separate, and this time he made it a point of telling me that he thought he no longer loved me. I cried, begged, literally crawled to make him reconsider but there was no way he wanted anything to do with me and he simply left.

It was then that I started to seek God, but without much understanding of how. It was the first time that I really approached God in my life.

How did God change your situation, Camille, as you sought Him wholeheartedly?

Dear brides, I'm hoping to share my testimony with you and give you as many details as I can in order to encourage you because the testimonies that are full of details have helped me too. However, it is not my desire to expose my husband's sins, so I promise that I will soon tell you how bad a wife I was. I want you to know what you read here at RMI, where it says that even if your husband comes home that he won't stay for long is true! If God is not with you or if there is no transformation that's what will happen to you. BELIEVE ME he'll leave again and again and again because I lived it!

I knew what I had to do this time. I knew there was only one way to change the way I was and it began when I was looking for God! Not knowing what to do, I went to my local church and talked to my pastor's wife (a sweet woman, who did her best to help me when all I could do was cry). So I basically found an ePartner during the first days of the destruction, but I needed more. I needed to know whether or not God was going to restore my marriage. I doubted He would because I heard from everyone "perhaps God was preparing a better man for me" so my emotions and thoughts were divided. Should I pray for the restoration of my marriage or pray for a new husband who is better suited for me? In the midst of my despair, I prayed to God and asked. I begged Him to show me because I wanted the restoration of my marriage, but I needed to know if God wanted it too.

By this time, my husband had already been gone for two months and the pain was killing me. It was then, in answer to prayer, that I discovered RMI. A kind woman from another state, who I didn't even know saw my prayer request and sent me a message with the HopeAtLast.com link and Chapter 1 of the book, *How God Can and Will Restore Your Marriage*! I couldn't believe it when I read that message, God answered me, Hallelujah! He did hear me when I prayed and He was confirming what He wanted for me. He wanted to restore my marriage: He was very clear!

Immediately, I started reading the book, then I devoured everything that was on the website. I began working through the courses, journaling every step I took on my journey and started submitting praise reports of my own. My mind and heart were being transformed and from that moment on I knew there was hope!

What principles, from God's Word (or through our resources), Camille, did the Lord teach you during this trial?

I absorbed as much as I could and will continue to absorb for as long as I live. I first learned how much of a contentious woman that I was. When I read that title, A Contentious Woman, in one of the early chapters of the book *How God Can and Will Restore Your Marriage*, I thought proudly, "Well, this chapter is not meant for me, I am not quarrelsome or anything close." Oh, how wrong I was.

As I read the book, God convinced me that it was His will to restore my marriage. And that it was He who removed my husband so that I would totally turn to God. I learned to seek the love of my Heavenly Husband. I'd never heard of this before, but I wanted it to help stop the pain. It is almost impossible to believe that I could be His Bride and experience this kind of love so many testimonies talked about.

But above all, God showed me how wrong I was and what a wretched wife I was to my husband. I never let my husband be the head of my house, everything had to be my way. I felt superior to him because I had no addictions (alcohol, drugs, etc.) and also because I have a higher education and he only just finished high school. I believed myself to be the one who knew more and actually believed he was lucky to have me. The more I read the book, the more God convicted me and showed me everything, absolutely everything wrong that I had done over the nine years we have been together as a couple. That's when I stopped looking at my husband's shortcoming and I knew I needed to change. It all depended on my relationship with my HH.

What were the most difficult times that God helped you through, Camille?

The most difficult time for me was the very beginning when I found out that my EH was with an OW. A deep piercing pain entered my chest and remained there until I was truly my HH's Bride. Back then, I walked around the house because I couldn't sit still. I hated the weekends because I was alone at home (since we don't have any children). However, when I found RMI, I started to love staying at home alone. I had time to be with my Beloved HH. But the weekends that were horrible happened in the first two months, which later became wonderful, all due to the time I spent with my HH.

Another difficult moment, but one that God prepared me for (because when we entrust everything to God He prepares us for upcoming storms), was when my EH told me through a text message that he was pretty sure that OW was pregnant. I was at my job, so I grabbed my 3x5 cards from my desk where I had written down the Word of God and I went to the bathroom and began reading them. I got to Psalms 112:7, "You will not fear bad news; your heart is steadfast, trusting in the Lord." When I got home later that day, I searched the Bible on the internet for words about children and conception and God gave me the promise, Hosea 9:11 "As for Ephraim, their glory will fly away like a bird— No birth, no pregnancy and no conception!" I added it to pile my 3x5 cards and clung to that promise and prayed it over and over and God honored it, the OW was not pregnant. Hallelujah!

Camille, what was the "turning point" of your restoration?

When I finally learned to let my EH go. It took time for me to learn this principle. But I started asking God to help me forget my EH. I asked God to make my HH be the love of my life, to be my First Love as described in His Word.

So I didn't expect my EH to be back even though we were talking almost every day, as it still seemed that everything was going wonderfully with OW. Yet I was sure that God would restore my marriage but I didn't know it would happen so fast and come out of nowhere!

We've all heard that "God answers all of our prayers" and this is so true! At the beginning of my journey, I prayed and asked God to restore my marriage as quickly as possible. I even prayed and asked Him to restore before the end of the year, because I did not want to spend Christmas and New Year, away from my EH. But I began to get excited to spend the holidays and the New Year alone with the Lord. When I told Him "let it be done according to His will" He granted my heart's desire! I spent time alone with my HH and then God also knew I was ready for Him to restore my marriage and for my EH to return home.

Tell us HOW it happened, Camille? Did your husband just walk in the front door? Camille, did you suspect or could you tell you were close to being restored?

On a Wednesday night, just after the first of the year, my EH sent me a message asking if he could come home. I, immediately texted back, "Yes, of course." However, after I agreed, the question arose in my heart if I really wanted him back. I was so close to my HH, my life was perfect. But I knew that telling him not to come wasn't His plan. Knowing too, how things were never good when he came back before, made me question if this was a good or a bad thing. Once I spoke to my HH, I knew that everything would be okay because this time it was different from the other times, this time it was God who brought my EH home and not me!

I simply had a great certainty in my heart that the Lord had great plans for me and my EH. But no, it was not easy, as in the lessons and testimonies I read said happens. I am so thankful I had enough time to get through all the courses so I could be prepared to welcome my EH home and weather the storms after he returned.

When he came in he didn't ask me for forgiveness nor did he say he loved me or anything. There was nothing romantic whatsoever. he simply said that he and the OW were fighting a lot (in the lessons, Erin says that even though the other side seems like a paradise this is not true, sin never brings happiness) and that he decided it would be better to be with me than her. Immediately, I remembered it says exactly that. from the prayer I'd prayed from the RYM book!

"Therefore I will hedge up his way with thorns, and I will build a wall against him so that he cannot find his paths. And he will pursue his lovers, but will not overtake them; and he will seek them, but will not find them. Then he will say, 'I will go back to my wife. For it was better for me then than now!' Therefore I will allure him, bring him into the wilderness, and speak kindly to him. For I will remove the names of Baals from his mouth. Then the Lord said to me, 'Go again, love a (man) yet an adulterer.'" From Hosea 2.

So I again, I knew it was God, and simply didn't bother him. I just let him say what he wanted to share, while I made sure I was responding with my new gentle and quiet spirit. I took this time to fall in love with my HH again and chose to get away to be alone with Him. Not hovering around my EH but in a way looking disinterested ultimately led to my husband pursuing me. Now he's romantic and kind with me again.

Would you recommend any of our resources in particular that helped you, Camille?

I recommend ALL the materials. I tell everyone just read the book, *How God Can and Will Restore Your Marriage,* because every married woman should read it. Share it with people because this gives everyone a lot of hope and to be able to recognize God's will for their lives. It also shows you how wrong you are, the way you are living now. *A Wise Woman* really helped me a lot in this area of my life. I also recommend the courses, many of the questions you have will be answered and it will all begin to make sense. I recommend all of Erin's Be Encouraged eVideos, they are wonderful and will show the steps taken by this wise sister who gave up her life to help you.

Would you be interested in helping encourage other women, Camille?

Yes, I'd love to!

Either way, Camille, what kind of encouragement would you like to leave women with, in conclusion?

When I read in the other testimonies "do not give up" my heart was filled with joy! Oh, how many times I cried when reading testimonies of restoration and them ending with "do not give up." Today, for the Glory of God I am here saying the same thing to all of you, dear brides. Will God restore your marriage? Yes, oh yes! As difficult and as impossible as it may seem, God will do it! But it depends exclusively on you, it is all about your relationship with God, then finding your HH and trusting Him with everything. He knows bringing your husband back will just mean he will go again and again and again. But with the way He wants to transform you along your journey, that's when He knows your ready and He is able to grant you your heart's desire— just as He did with me!

Chapter 35

Ophelia

"For He rescued us from the domain of darkness,
and transferred us to the kingdom of His beloved Son,
in whom we have redemption, the forgiveness of sins."
—Colossians 1:13-14

"Our Prince Charming"

Ophelia, how did your restoration actually begin?

My relationship with my husband has never been stable ever since we began dating. Several times we broke up and got back together. But the last time we broke up he promised me he would change and that's when we started attending a church and that led to us deciding to get married in the church. But even after we married and even though we weren't living in sin anymore we had an unstable and tumultuous relationship.

After we got married, everything only got worse, the fights grew violent, and soon he despised me. I only looked at his sins which increased the distance between us. Everyone who was close to us talked about us and about our marriage, including everyone in our church. And to make matters worse, his mother came to live with us because her husband (my husband's stepfather) kicked her out. Even before she arrived I knew it was the beginning of the end.

We moved to a larger apartment to accommodate his mother, but it only got worse, because we were both full of hatred, resentment and everything got scary. It was a dark time in our relationship.

That was when my accusations started. I was so angry when I noticed he stopped wearing his wedding ring, and when I'd challenge him, he vowed to file for separation if I didn't stop. We fought a lot, continuously, but I never thought that it would end with us really breaking up. I thought because I worked hard to make sure everything worked out, it would. What a mistake to think he would just want to keep living this nightmare.

We soon moved into a house, so I thought we were secure, we would not be separating, but a few days later just after moving in, he left the house and went to stay at his brother's house. I had already found the RYM book on the internet and began practicing the principles of the book, so I did not suffer as much as I would have. I realized My Love had prepared me for what He knew was coming. What hurt me most were the attacks from the enemy coming from my own husband.

How did God change your situation, Ophelia, as you sought Him wholeheartedly?

As I said I was already applying the principles from RYM. I had already surrendered to God and His will. God lovingly showed how unfaithful I was to Him, as well as how contentious, quarrelsome, accusing, and judgemental I was as a wife. In short, I was a full-blown Pharisee. He showed me all my sins and I sought Him to be clean. He forgave my sins and called me to repentance and confess to those I'd hurt.

I asked for forgiveness from the people I humiliated and hurt with my spiritual and carnal arrogance. God brought me out of the darkness and showed me that I belonged to Him. I could be more than just a good wife, I could be His bride. He took the darkness out of me in an amazing way. Day after day the trials intensified but with each trial, I became closer and closer to Him. He taught me to take care of myself, take care of the house (using *workers@home*), and finally teaching me to submit to my authorities because I was always a rebel.

The more I sought Him with all my heart, the more I read the lessons and journaled, the more I submitted accounts of praise, the more I read the Bible, the more intimate My Love and I became. I have never been so well cared for, protected, loved, and utterly at peace. He is My Everything.

What principles, from God's Word (or through our resources), Ophelia, did the Lord teach you during this trial?

The Lord is still teaching me because although my earthly husband has returned, he has not returned or been restored to the Lord. For many weeks we were not even intimate. I began writing my testimony and was actually waiting because I was not sure if it would be a true testimony of a restored marriage. So in faith I began to write it and asked Him to confirm that He had indeed restored us. God was again faithful when He brought me through another adverse situation, a doozy of a trial. This time my husband didn't send me away, nor did he leave. I remained gentle and quiet and God took care of everything. Only then did I realize that our marriage had indeed been restored!

My Heavenly Love taught me to take responsibility for my mistakes, my failures, to recognize and simply ask for forgiveness. My Heavenly Love taught me to take care of my home and my family, to let go of everything: my husband and let go of my church. My Heavenly Love taught me not to be angry, but to take every thought captive and discuss the matter with Him, to close my mouth and only just share how I feel to Him. And my Heavenly Love taught me to trust and wait on Him.

My Heavenly Love taught me to make Him My All in All, that if I have Him I have everything and He is enough for me. He taught me to delight in Him, that nothing we see or hear is true because the Truth is Only One thing. Truth is Him and His Word.

What were the most difficult times that God helped you through, Ophelia?

There were several difficult moments, but the most difficult for me was letting go. As everyone says, it was very painful and difficult, especially letting go after you're restored. I have to do it every day with my husband now that he is at home. To simply trust Him to work it out.

Also, the attacks from the enemy through social networks were very painful. Reading my husband's words about how he was living really hurt me a lot. Thankfully I went to My Beloved to cry and cry. That's when He also instructed me to delete my EH's contacts from my cell phone, delete my account from Facebook and block him from my Whatsapp. Basically to entirely let go of any temptation and disappear from everyone. I know this had a lot to do with him coming to try to find me again. I wish I'd done it sooner but I was afraid if I let go to this degree he might never come back, but the opposite was true.

Ophelia, what was the "turning point" of your restoration?

The turning point was when I told Him that He IS bigger than everything, bigger than the whole situation that I was going through, that my bills would be paid by Him because I tithed to my storehouse, that He is with me and taking care of me, so I don't need anything more from anyone, because He is My Everything. And that I didn't want my husband or my marriage restored anymore, that after I listed the pros and cons of having a restored marriage I was able to finally decide that My Love was obviously much better, nor can He be compared to any man on earth. And that I chose My Love over being restored.

Tell us HOW it happened, Ophelia? Did your husband just walk in the front door? Ophelia, did you suspect or could you tell you were close to being restored?

My husband said a lot of times that he was thinking of coming back, but he always said horrible things afterward. I watched God as He began to turn his heart to come back and since we don't have children, the only thing that united us was my desire for My Love and nothing else. Women without children always wonder what will cause their husbands to return, but He proved to me this truth that nothing is impossible with Him and He has a plan.

My EH began to call to see if I wanted to go get something to eat, which was the answer to my prayer that I'd applied. Asking My Love to show him our happy moments and I didn't even know it was eating out! But My Love knew! Next, as an excuse to see me he started bringing our dog for me to see (without me asking).

Our occasional dating and him visiting me lasted for a month, and during this time he even told me more than once that he would come home. But because he said it, but didn't come back, I didn't really believe it. Besides, I no longer wanted restoration. The day after I poured my heart out to My Love (that I mentioned above with Him being all I wanted or needed) was when he came home. And although he had a house key, he waited outside for me to be home to come from work. At first, he slept in the guest room, but after a week he returned to our bed. I knew that each step was God doing what He does. "Like rivers of water, so is the heart of the king in the hand of the Lord, who inclines him to do His will." Proverbs 21:1

MY ETERNAL AND ONLY LOVE. I LOVE YOU, I LOVE YOU, I LOVE YOU, YOU ARE EVERYTHING I WANT, YOU ARE EVERYTHING I NEED, YOU ARE MY REASON FOR LIVING.

Would you recommend any of our resources in particular that helped you with your restored marriage, Ophelia?

Yes, the book *How God Can and Will Restore Your Marriage* is what made the difference for me and it was knowing what I read on the cover that Erin had already been there. The course, along with the forms to allow me to journal and write my thoughts and concerns to Him helped so much. Also, the Be E videos, reading and submitting the praise reports, which help when we are almost hopeless, especially when you read your own praise on the blog! I really enjoyed reading A wise woman and also all of the abundant life books that help me keep My Love first in my life.

Would you be interested in helping encourage other women, Ophelia?

Yes, I certainly want to help other women, being a channel of the Lord and give women hope.

Either way, Ophelia, what kind of encouragement would you like to leave women with, in conclusion?

Do not believe in anything that you see or hear, trust only in the Lord, nothing is impossible for God, if you lean on Him.

"Delight in the Lord also, and He will grant you the desires of your heart." Psalms 37:4.

Do not believe in "free will", there is no will but God's. He is greater than everything, He took your husband from you, everything was His permission.

"Like streams of water like this is the heart of the king in the hand of the Lord, who inclines him to all his will". Proverbs 21:1.

A man's heart plans his way, but the Lord directs his steps. Proverbs 16:9.

Man's steps are directed by the Lord; how, then, will man understand his way? Proverbs 20:24.

Make no mistake He IS King, and reigns Unique and Sovereign, He IS the MAN, our Prince Charming. He is who Lives and Reigns and spoils us as His beloved bride.

Chapter 36

Tiara

"Rejoice in the Lord always; again I will say, rejoice!
Let your gentle spirit be known to all men.
The Lord is near. Be anxious for nothing,
but in everything by prayer and supplication
with thanksgiving let your requests be made known to God."
—Philippians 4:4-6

"My Husband Lived a "Single" Life"

Tiara, how did your restoration actually begin?

"Delight in the Lord"

My beloved sisters in Christ. First of all, I want to praise God for His love and mercy in my life and I give Him all the honor and glory for my testimony.

I also want to apologize for the delay in sending my testimony, I kept putting it off because I wanted to send a testimony of a restored marriage from my perspective, but now I understand that everything must be from God's perspective and not mine.

For a long time I was foolish and helped considerably to destroy my home. Both us worked and lived in different cities and saw each other only on the weekends. When I got pregnant with our son I thought God had answered my prayer because I wanted us to be living together again. My husband said he wanted us together again, so much too, so I thought this was it.

Our plans were that when my maternity leave ended I would quit my job and we'd finally live together. But when my maternity leave ended, my husband insisted that I not resign, as we were building a house and the job market was bad and that it only would be for "just a little longer." So, I went back to the place where I worked when my son was

5-month-old and after a while a mutual friend of ours started to alert me that my husband was getting involved with an OW, a co-worker.

At first I didn't believe it, because I thought he had what he wanted most; he wanted a family. But as time passed I noticed some changes in our relationship.

It got worse and the changes were more noticeable when I up and left my job and went to live with him. That's when I knew he was really getting involved with the OW, which was confirmed the day I saw an exchange of messages from both of them on his cell phone. When I read it I dropped to the ground and hit my head. My mind was reeling from reading such intimate details I wish I'd never seen. That night we fought a lot and what I did most was to offend him so that he could feel some of the pain I was feeling.

In the middle of our discussion, after the fighting, he told me that he no longer loved me as before and that all this distance from us living apart, along with my bossy ways and the times that I said no when he first asked me to be together and live in the same city (but it would have meant me changing jobs so I refused) all contributed to the end of his love for me. He said he had gotten used to living another kind of life and by this time, with me asking him to think about our baby who was innocent and didn't deserve all of this happening to him, it was too late. Through intense ongoing pressure, my husband finally gave in and said that we would try again, but only for the sake of our son.

I remember crying and asking God to save my marriage and I believe that at that very moment God started working on my heart to trust Him for my marriage.

But, I still didn't have enough wisdom (I had even started to change my behavior). And even though a Christian friend helped me through prayer and advice, after a few days when everything had surfaced, I couldn't stand it and left our home (never do that, that's all the enemy wants). I took my son and went to live with my mother in our hometown about 700 miles away from our home where my husband was living and working. After about 15 days, I returned to my hometown to live closer. He came to visit us and we resumed to make an attempt to rescue our marriage a second time. But, he insisted that my son and I remain where we were and if I left and moved away again, it would be over for good.

How did God change your situation, Tiara, as you sought Him wholeheartedly?

When I found myself in this situation of losing my family, I felt that only God could transform all this pain and change this situation that seemed utterly impossible due to my husband's harsh words and coldness towards me.

So I called on Him to help me and I started looking on the internet for marriage restoration and found the RYM book and your website. I ordered the eBook and downloaded it to my phone and when I read it was then that I realized how foolish I was for so many years. I realized I had torn my marriage down. I was selfish, things always had to be my way. But, thanks to our Beloved, in His infinite mercy He took me from the quicksand where I was and opened my eyes to the truth, which is His Word and placed me on the Rock. The truth as it says in His Word, it sets us free and I am so grateful for that.

With God everything is possible! Today I am a new woman. I know I still need to change, but my Darling is shaping me every day, all glory and praise for Him. God is shaping us all and as this happens our situation is transformed, because He makes all things work together for our good.

What principles, from God's Word (or through our resources), Tiara, did the Lord teach you during this trial?

We must put God first in our lives, we must cry out to Him and cry for Him only. We cannot cry for our husband. He must be who we want. I tried to follow the principles in the *How God Can and Will Restore Your Marriage* book, but until He was my HH I would change but change back again. This book is wonderful and clear to know more about the Word of God and to hold on to His Promises for my life. But it was learning to live abundantly that I changed inside and supernaturally began to follow the principles without even trying.

Fasting and prayers helped me, to humble me, and still helps me a lot to keep my gentle and quiet spirit. It is also necessary to put on all spiritual weapons and of course the Word of God.

What were the most difficult times that God helped you through, Tiara?

The most difficult times were when my son and I stayed in our hometown while my husband lived a "single" life. It hurt my heart and I had many nights of crying, where I cried out to God on my knees to remove this suffering. At all times, I felt His Presence comforting me and giving me strength to continue for the Glory of His Kingdom.

It was during the most painful moments of my Journey when I realized God was always by my side and when I thought about giving up, He told me to believe Him for my marriage.

Tiara, what was the "turning point" of your restoration?

The turning point was when I started to depend more on God and less on my husband. And God in His infinite power began to orchestrate everything in my favor. I had a lot of difficulty to stop fighting in the flesh, so I saw that the more I stopped fighting in the flesh, the more God acted in my favor. So sisters, let God be God so that things will start to flow. I started praising Him in all situations and that totally changed the spiritual atmosphere in my home and life.

And I surrendered my future and that of my son to my HH so that it could be done according to His Will. Let it be said in passing that His will, His plan is so much better than ours.

"Rejoice in the Lord always. Again I will say: rejoice! Let your kindness be known to all. The Lord is near. Do not be anxious about anything, but in everything, in prayer and supplications, and with thanksgiving, submit your requests to God." Philippians 4:4-6.

Tell us HOW it happened, Tiara? Did your husband just walk in the front door? Tiara, did you suspect or could you tell you were close to being restored?

One morning I received the news that my husband had been fired and the OW had also been let go. My husband called me a day later to say that he had been fired (he didn't comment on the other person's dismissal and I didn't ask anything either) and that he was returning to our hometown. I praised God, because I knew it was His acting and restoration must be His plan.

Reading a lesson that day, I was able to see how real what Sister Erin is telling us about the return of our husbands, coming home after a crisis hits. When my husband returned to our home and hometown, it was not as I expected. He was not a man transformed nor did he ask for forgiveness.

It is as Erin tells us, in the beginning there is no way you want this restored marriage, but as each day passes, you begin to see God completing what He started (as long as you don't go back to the way you would have handled each crisis). As I kept my HH first, which isn't easy but I snuck away to be intimate with Him, I began to see many changes in my husband's behavior. He began making plans for our future. Again, I know that God will finish what He started and that it is God, not us who restores. He is in control of the situation. Only God could have orchestrated what led to my restoration: my husband returned back home, after he was fired, and what led to him also not having contact with the OW or wanting contact because she is what caused him to be fired (which I learned later). I know it was God who allowed this to happen and got him out of that place in his life so we could be restored and start over.

That was one of the answers to one of my prayers, I asked God to build a hedge of thorns around my husband and get him out of that city and that job so that we could be together as a family.

"Like streams of water like this is the heart of the king in the hand of the Lord, who inclines him to all his will." Proverbs 21:1.

"Delight yourself also in the Lord, and he will grant you the desires of your heart." Psalm 37:4.

"Therefore, behold, I will surround your way with thorns; and I will erect a wall of hedge, lest she find her paths. She will go after her lovers, but she will not reach them; and she will seek them, but not them. she will find it, then she will say: I will go, and I will become my first husband, because I was better off then than now." Hosea 2:6-7.

Would you recommend any of our resources in particular that helped you, Tiara?

Yes, the book *How God Can and Will Restore Your Marriage*, Daily Encourager, Devotionals, Courses and also the book *A Wise Woman*, which I am reading now.

These resources are a blessing for us who are thirsty for truth and for real change in our lives.

Would you be interested in helping encourage other women, Tiara?

Yes, I really want to be able to help other women.

Either way, Tiara, what kind of encouragement would you like to leave women with, in conclusion?

My dear sisters in Christ, never give up on your families. For our God is a God of truth and makes the impossible happen. He is faithful to fulfill every Promise that has been promised to us. So take advantage of this moment in your journey to delight in the Lord.

I will be praying for all of you and already with certainty, can see the victory for each one of you. ;)

"Commit your way to the Lord; trust him, and he will do everything." Psalm 37:5.

Chapter 37

Josefa

"And He said to him, 'you shall love the
Lord your God with all your heart,
and with all your soul, and with all your mind.'"
—Matthew 22:37

"Let Him be Who You Need in Your Life!!"

Josefa, how did your restoration actually begin?

Well, I always had problems with jealousy, and early this year there were so many changes happening in my job. Times when I suffered injustice and ended up going to work at night to avoid the conflicts happening during the day shift. Soon I just became bitter and moody. My life became a cycle of complaining about my boss and whining about how bad my life was. As I started to be alone all day, because I worked the night shift, I started thinking only about my husband, and I started to obsess over him, accusing him of not loving me anymore, of not paying attention to me enough, until the day he was at work, and I began pestering him with a series of annoying messages. Because he was busy dealing with me, he was given a warning at work. That night he packed up his things, told me he blocked me on his phone and walked out of the house, saying that because I complained so much that he didn't love me anymore and probably never did love me. The last thing he shouted before slamming the door was "Just leave me alone!!!"

How did God change your situation, Josefa, as you sought Him wholeheartedly?

In the beginning, like all of the restored marriage testimonies I've read, I prayed all the time for restoration after he walked out. I soon discovered RMI when someone shared RMI and HopeAtLast.com on a Facebook post. It wasn't even a response to what I posted, I just saw someone else ask and a friend of mine replied to her! The next day I gathered a group of women from my country to begin studying the RYM as we each started our own Restoration Journeys.

It wasn't long before I read a post in the Encourager that I began to look for my own personal restoration. I started wanting to love the Lord with all my heart. I started asking Him to allow me to find the peace that surpasses all understanding because I didn't want to live according to the circumstances as I always lived, and the way things were happening in my life. Little by little I stopped counting the days in the desert and I started to enjoy the moments at home alone with our beautiful Lord. Once He became my HH and I was really a bride, I switched from a Restoration Journey to an Abundant Life Journey!

What principles, from God's Word (or through our resources), Josefa, did the Lord teach you during this trial?

Reading and knowing the Word makes all the difference! When you have a problem every single person around you will give you stupid advice to feed your flesh. Instead, I applied everything I learned, and the first thing was taking everything to God first. Next was being faithful to tithe to my storehouse after I let go of my church. I began praising God even when everything seems to fall apart. Also never speaking ill of my husband to other people. Last was when I chose to obey and submit to my husband's authority even during the separation.

God really tested me when I had to obey to the point of buying a car for my husband, in my name! We only had one car, which I kept when I moved out. And due to some restrictions, he couldn't put it in his name so he asked me for this favor. In my head, it seemed that everything was beginning to get worse because now he would have a car to have fun and live a life as a bachelor. It got worse when I began hearing that he was going from one OW to the next, moving in and "living the life." Nevertheless, I chose to trust God and His Word, and today I am the one driving in that car with him!

What were the most difficult times that God helped you through, Josefa?

The most difficult times were the weekends when there was nothing but solitude at home, but God used it for good. He was showing me that He was there with me. Soon I started to leave the house and we'd do things, just me and my Beloved.

Another thing that bothered me a lot was seeing my husband sometimes on my street because he came back to live at my mother-in-law's house after he tired of living with OWs. So we lived in the same neighborhood. It was difficult when I came home and I'd see him hanging out. All I did was take it to my HH, saying that I didn't want to see him walking around without his "other half" because we are one flesh. Soon He answered this concern too, now no one sees us apart.

Josefa, what was the "turning point" of your restoration?

It began when I started resting in God! I started not to look at my situation and I started to be grateful for everything I had. I made new friends who were also trusting God for restoration for their marriages and then shifting to just wanting Him. When I learned to give myself totally to my HH, leaving my restoration to God to restore "if it was His will" and allowing Him to change in me in every way that did not please Him. I believe the final turning point was when I adamantly did not want to be restored. It's almost if God was waiting and said to my HH, "Okay, now she's ready" hahaha.

Tell us HOW it happened, Josefa? Did your husband just walk in the front door? Josefa, did you suspect or could you tell you were close to being restored?

My husband had made new "friends" at work, all were separated and who wanted to live the life of teenagers, living together, playing video games, being with women, etc. I prayed a lot that God would show him that this was not the life that would take him anywhere and God did what I'd asked!

While on a holiday, my husband invited me to have lunch with him and my in-laws, and that's when he told me that he wanted to try again. At first, he didn't want to come back home, he just wanted us to be boyfriend and girlfriend. Because I knew we needed to change as a couple, I trusted God and accepted. At first, it hurt me that he called me his girlfriend and that he'd come to our house but then leave to go sleep at his parents' house. Several times I had to bite my tongue in order not to demand anything from him, and perhaps that was my greatest test. I had to not care.

This continued for a few weeks, but as soon as I turned my attention from my EH again and remained focused on my Lover is when he started to sleep at home and gradually returned back each time bringing his clothes. This transition was perfect because I was able to keep my HH first and have enough time to be alone with Him.

Would you recommend any of our resources in particular that helped you, Josefa?

Yes, I read the books *How God Can and Will Restore Your Marriage, A Wise Woman, Questions and Answers,* and I also took one RMI courses every day and watched the Be Encouraged videos more than once a day from my phone. I got to know the RMTs and what restoration really looked like and what triggered it to happen—being His alone.

Would you be interested in helping encourage other women, Josefa?

Certainly! We must comfort others with the comfort we have received from Him!

Either way, Josefa, what kind of encouragement would you like to leave women with, in conclusion?

Beloved ones, believe in God alone! From that, you will be able to rest and start looking for Him the way He wants to be found! I, particularly, could not find Him as my Heavenly Husband, but because at the age of 9 I lost my father, who was the most upright man I have ever met. So when I met the Lord, God came to meet my needs so I'd have a caring father, a Heavenly Father. For me, I decided to continue that way, which was what I always needed the most. That's when I realized He could become my Heavenly Love and I found the comfort I needed. So seek God with all your heart and allow Him to speak to your hearts and the rest He will do it! Let Him be who you need in your life.

Chapter 38

Charlotte

"Therefore I am well content with weaknesses,
with insults, with distresses,
with persecutions, with difficulties, for Christ's sake;
for when I am weak, then I am strong."
—2 Corinthians 12:10

"A Simple Wedding in a Chapel"

Charlotte, how did your restoration actually begin?

I was divorced for almost a year, but in the beginning I did not want my marriage restored—I wanted a divorce, and I followed that painful route for my life. I had another relationship with someone I'd met while I was married to my husband. My ex-husband also followed this same path for his life, he, too, had several other relationships after we divorced. At the time, I knew God, but I was far from being a believer or follower, even though I called myself a Christian.

Then one day, by the grace of God, He turned my heart back to my husband. The first step was to go back to God, and so I did. After this, the desire to have my marriage restored became even stronger. That's when I began my restoration journey.

After so long (and it was me who cheated and divorced my husband for another man), it seemed crazy to everyone when I actually became desperate for restoration. I simply had no idea how to get my husband and marriage back. I had to face the truth that it was impossible, which is when a friend who began praying with me sent me the paperback book *How God Can and Will Restore Your Marriage*. I started reading, and for the first time I had hope.

What I didn't know is that my husband was no longer in a relationship with any other woman, but he had in fact come under deep conviction, knowing his lifestyle was wrong in God's eyes. He had joined a men's group at a church, and it was there that someone gave him the men's *Restore Your Marriage*.

How did God change your situation, Charlotte, as you sought Him wholeheartedly?

What happened is that God began to work, but not in my marriage, in me. Of course, today I understand why, but at the time it made no sense. Changing me, introducing me to the RYM and then the website, I learned so much. I came to know Him as my HH. Gently and lovingly, He showed me how wrong I was, how I was a foolish, contentious woman who tore her house down, and how (by living in sin), I had turned completely away from God—which was the worst decision I have ever made in my life.

Soon, I began to understand that all that was happening was His plan. God turned my heart, gave me a desire for my marriage, so that I would turn to Him, so that I would truly love Him above all things, and it worked! Dear Reader, this process lasted for 4 months, but it seemed like years, because I cried a lot. I suffered in a way I had never suffered. The journey was not easy, but it was invaluable at making me a different woman entirely.

What principles, from God's Word (or through our resources), Charlotte, did the Lord teach you during this trial?

I learned a lot from the trials. I learned to trust God all the time, to rest in Him and to know that He cares for me more than I'd ever imagined, so I was able to entrust my life and my daughters to Him. The most astonishing thing was how He took care of us. Soon after He called me on this journey, I lost my job and the unemployment benefits barely covered any of our needs. Yet, when I asked my Heavenly Husband or Heavenly Father—God made sure we were never once lacking in anything we needed.

During this, I read the Word of God; I fasted; I prayed, and I had so many wonderful hours with my HH that would not have been possible if I had been employed at the time!

What were the most difficult times that God helped you through, Charlotte?

The hardest time was when I applied "letting go," because just after he turned my heart, my EH began calling to talk to our daughters, and it made me sad, because as soon as my heart wanted to see and spend time with him, I needed to let go. And as I did, it seemed that the more I prayed the more complicated things had become.

Soon after this, my ex began coming to stay all weekend to see our daughters. Neither of us spoke to the other, but my heart was hurting. I knew the Lord was in control, which calmed my heart and helped me to rest in HIM. It was not easy, but it worked, and thank God I met a woman whose marriage had been restored, sent to me by God, who helped me focus on my own journey and not focus on what was happening around me.

At the time, I had no idea my ex had been hoping for restoration and was also letting go, focusing on becoming the man of God and spiritual leader of our family.

Charlotte, what was the "turning point" of your restoration?

It's when I really and truly let go. When I decided to make that decision, that very day I told my daughters that when dad called they should only tell me if there was something I needed to know (because prior to this, they made it a point of telling me everything, and I asked many questions).

I knew it was going to be hard for me to let go each weekend, to win my husband without a word, but God help me and show me how to act when he was there, but my HH also gave me a way of escape, when I was invited to stay at a friend's cabin that was almost like a honeymoon retreat for my HH and me. This actually happened two weekends in a row, with me gone when he came to see our daughters, so we spent almost three weeks without seeing each other or talking to each other.

It all changed on our oldest daughter's 19th birthday, when my youngest daughter asked if we could invite her father to come to her birthday party. My daughter said he immediately said he'd love to come, which was such a surprise, as it was scheduled for Sunday, and he always said he had to be at church, that he could not come because he led a Bible study and worship. So I honestly did not expect him to come. On her birthday, when he arrived at the door of the house, I greeted him, and when I hugged him, he started crying. I got worried and asked what had happened, but he said nothing.

A few minutes later, I saw him sitting in my room, on the bed, and felt led to go ask him if he was okay. What he said shocked me. He said that from the moment he stepped onto the doorstep, he felt the presence of God so strongly, just like it had been at a revival he'd recently attended. That's when he told me how much he'd missed me, missed being a family, missed us all living together! After the party, he slept at home, but as we were divorced, he slept in the guest bedroom and not with me. But I knew we were close, very close, to restoration. I just needed to wait and watch what God planned to do next.

Tell us HOW it happened, Charlotte. Did your husband just walk in the front door? Charlotte, did you suspect or could you tell you were close to being restored?

Yes, I knew I was close, with everything that had happened at the birthday party, but I prepared myself for some testing.

I heard that he'd moved out of his apartment and was staying with his mother, because she can't be alone for too long. So after work, he'd go get her fed, but then he came straight over here every day for a few weeks. At first, he focused on seeing the girls and almost ignored me. I knew it was my test, so I chose to get closer to my HH and often left just to get a coffee or go for a walk with Him. That's when my ex began talking to me again. We began talking a lot, and soon we began talking about our wedding and getting married again.

We decided on a simple wedding in a chapel, with just our daughters and a few family members who had been supportive also in attendance. We were both different people than the couple who married so many years before. I had a gentle and quiet spirit and my husband was a true man of God.

Would you recommend any of our resources in particular that helped you, Charlotte?

How God Can and Will Restore Your Marriage and each of the testimonies were great to read, and they were what inspired me to keep going and helped give me strength to continue. Of course, the Word of God is unmatched.

And Erin, if you ever read this, I am very grateful to God for your life, for helping you through your journey, for your love for your neighbor, me, and all the many marriages that have been restored and lives like mine changed. I praise God for your life!

Would you be interested in helping encourage other women, Charlotte?

Yes

Either way, Charlotte, what kind of encouragement would you like to leave women with, in conclusion?

Trust in God, and make sure you give everything to Him, because even when everything seems to be going wrong (because you will have so many trials), you can be sure God is in control—the Creator of heaven and earth. He is the God who specializes in miracles, the God who truly loves you and will not let any harm happen to you. Just believe that even adversity will bring you contentment in the end. "For my power is made perfect in its weakness." Always trust, and do not give up, because restoration is a desire He put in your heart, and this desire in your heart is from God. Just believe and obey everything He commands. God is faithful. My testimony is proof.

What you have read is just a *small sample* of the POWER and FAITHFULNESS of God that are told through countless restored marriages! We continue to post new restored marriage, and restored relationship testimonies (children, siblings, parents, etc.) on our site each week.

Don't let ANYONE try to convince you that God cannot restore YOUR marriage! It is a lie. The TRUTH is that He is MORE THAN ABLE!!

Is Your Marriage... Crumbling? Hopeless? Or Ended in Divorce?

At Last There's Hope!

Have you been searching for marriage help online? It's not by chance, nor is it by coincidence, that you have this book in your hands. God is leading you to Restore Ministries that began by helping marriages that *appear* hopeless—like yours!

God has heard your cry for help in your marriage struggles and defeats. He predestined this **Divine Appointment** to give you the hope that you so desperately need right now!

We know and understand what you are going through since many of us in our restoration fellowship have a restored marriage and family! No matter what others have told you, your marriage is not hopeless! We know, after filling almost two books of restored marriage testimonies, that God is able to restore any marriage—especially yours!

"Behold, I am the LORD, the God of all flesh; is anything too difficult for Me?" (Jeremiah 32:27).

If you have been told that your marriage is hopeless or that without your husband's help your marriage cannot be restored! Each week we post a new Restored Relationship from one of our Restoration Fellowship Members that we post on our site.

"Ah Lord GOD! Behold, You have made the heavens and the earth by Your great power and by Your outstretched arm! Nothing is too difficult for You"! (Jeremiah 32:17).

If you have been crying out to God for more help, someone who understands, someone you can talk to, then we invite you to join our RMI Restoration Fellowship. Since beginning this fellowship, we have seen more marriages restored on a regular basis than we ever thought possible!

Restoration Fellowship

Restoration is a "narrow road"—look around, most marriages end in divorce! But if your desire is for a restored marriage, then our Restoration Fellowship is designed especially for you!

Since beginning this fellowship, we have seen marriages restored more consistently than we ever thought possible.

Let us help you stay committed to "working with God" to restore your marriages. Restoration Fellowship can offer you the help, guidance, and support you will need to stay on the path that leads to victory— *your* marriage restored!

Let us assure you that all of our marriages were restored by GOD (through His Word) as we sought Him to lead us, teach us, guide us and transform us through His Holy Spirit. This, too, is all you need for *your* marriage to be restored.

However, God continues to lead people to our ministry and fellowship to gain the faith, support and help that so many say that they needed in their time of crisis.

"I have tears in my eyes as I say I don't know what I would have done if I had not found this wonderful group of women. Thank you so much for all you do and may the Lord bless you and increase you in all you do!!!

Just read it and be open to what the Lord wants to change in your life

Each and every testimony has spoken to my heart and encouraged me that God can do for me what he has done for the Ladies who have a restored Marriage testimony praise God.

God used this ministry to show me that I was a contentious woman as well as manipulative and disobedient disrespectful. I realized that I had been the cause of my husband's desire to leave me. Now, whenever I see other women struggling in their marriage I love to direct them towards this website and pray that God will transform their lives as he did mine." Savanah in Texas

"The WOTT books were such a blessing to me. When I wasn't seeing progress in my own situation, I'd pick up my cell phone and open the downloaded books and just read. I would get so much hope from

hearing how even when it didn't look like it, even when it seemed impossible, God showed up and showed out for these believers. I recommend this book not only for you but for those around you. Once they read these testimonies, it will become a lot easier for them to stand in faith with you.

When I found you all, I was hopeless. I didn't know how to let go. I wanted to so badly because I could see that my grip was only making things worse. Talk about a hate wall. It seemed as high and even wider than the Great Wall of China. My EH was sooo angry with me. It had just been days since our first court appearance. And while I'd received Godly counsel early on not to get a lawyer unless I wanted a fight, I showed up and that resulted in the divorce being delayed. EH was so mad. He said that I was one who only manipulates and continues to attack him. God used the book and the courses to give me a true wake up call." Gianna in Kansas

Join our Restoration Fellowship TODAY and allow us to help YOU **restore** YOUR marriage.

HopeAtLast.com

Like What You've Read?

If you've been blessed by this book
get the full WOTT Series available
on EncouragingBookstore.com & Amazon.com

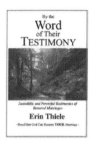

By the Word of Their Testimony (Book 1):
Incredible
and Powerful Testimonies of Restored Marriages

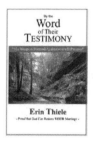

By the Word of Their Testimony (Book 2): No Weapon
Formed Against you will Prosper

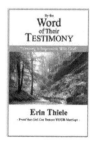

By the Word of Their Testimony (Book 3):
Nothing is Impossible With God

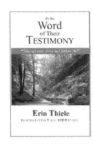

Word of Their Testimony (Book 4): Take up your cross and follow Me

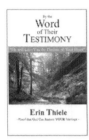

Word of Their Testimony (Book 5): He will Give You the Desires of Your Heart

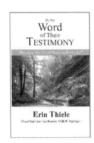

Word of Their Testimony (Book 6): Proclaim the Good News to Everyone

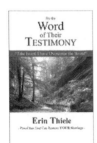

Word of Their Testimony (Book 7): Take Heart! I have Overcome the World

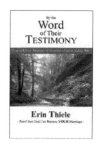

Word of Their Testimony (Book 8): You will
have Treasure in Heaven–Come, follow Me

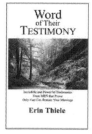

Word of Their Testimony: Incredible and
Powerful Testimonies of Restored Marriages
From Men

Also Available

on EncouragingBookstore.com & Amazon.com

For our Women

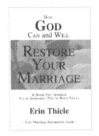

How God Can and Will Restore Your
Marriage: From Someone Who's Been There

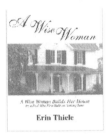

A Wise Woman: A Wise Woman Builds Her
House By a FOOL Who First Built on Sinking
Sand

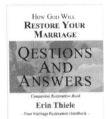

Questions and Answers: How God Will
Restore Your Marriage

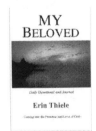

My Beloved: Daily Devotional and Journal

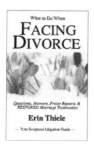

What to Do When Facing Divorce

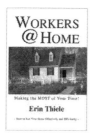

Workers@Home: Making the MOST of Your Time!

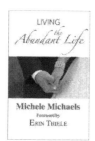

Facing Divorce —Again by Michele Michaels

Finding the Abundant Life by Michele Michaels

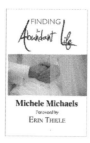

Living the Abundant Life by Michele Michaels

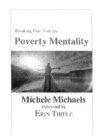

Breaking Free from the Poverty Mentality by
Michele Michaels

Each of our books is available on one of our websites as
FREE Courses!

For our Men

 How God Will Restore Your Marriage:
There's Healing After Broken Vows —A
Book for Men

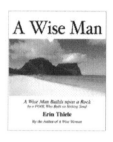 A Wise Man: A Wise Man Builds Upon a
Rock by a FOOL Who Built on Sinking Sand

Each of our books is available on one of our websites as
FREE Courses!

Restore Ministries International

POB 830 Ozark, MO 65721 USA

For more help
Please visit one of our Websites:

EncouragingWomen.org

HopeAtLast.com

LoveAtLast.org

RestoreMinistries.net

RMIEW.com

Aidemaritale.com (French)

AjudaMatrimonial.com (Portuguese)

AyudaMatrimonial.com (Spanish)

Eeuwigdurendeliefde-nl.com (Dutch)

EvliliginiKurtar.com (Turkish)

EternalLove-jp.com (Japanese)

Pag-asa.org (Filipino)

Uiteindelikhoop.com (Afrikaans)

Zachranamanzelstva.com (Slovakian)

Wiecznamilosc.com (Polish)

EncouragingMen.org

Where you'll also find FREE Courses for men and women.

Made in the USA
Middletown, DE
28 February 2023

25828913R00117